The Care Assistant's Handbook

Helen Howard

D1339884

AGE
Concern

BOOKS

© 2000 Helen Howard
Published by Age Concern England
1268 London Road
London SW16 4ER

First published 2000

Editor   Ro Lyon
Production   Vinnette Marshall
Design and typesetting   GreenGate Publishing Services
Printed in Great Britain by Bell & Bain Ltd, Glasgow

A catalogue record for this book is available from the British Library

ISBN 0–86242–288–4

All the case studies in the text are based on real case histories. The names and locations have been changed, however.

Bulk orders
Age Concern England is pleased to offer customised editions of all its titles to UK companies, institutions or other organisations wishing to make a bulk purchase. For further information, please contact the Publishing Department at the address on this page. Tel: 020 8765 7200. Fax: 020 8765 7211. E-mail: addisom@ace.org.uk

Contents

About the author   iv
Acknowledgements   v
Introduction   vi

1 Setting the Scene   1
2 Being New   11
3 A Day in the Life of a Care Assistant   26
4 Respecting Privacy and Dignity   40
5 Encouraging Independence   51
6 Valuing Individuality and Difference   63
7 Promoting Choice and Self-esteem   71
8 Recognising Rights and Responsibilities   80
9 Maintaining a Balance Between Safety and Risk   87
10 Health and Ageing   95
11 Getting Support and Feedback   104
12 What To Do When Things Go Wrong   113
13 Your Rights and Responsibilities   120

Appendix 1: Checklist of policies and procedures
             of care homes   132
Appendix 2: Sample activities programme   133
Appendix 3: Mapping the content against mandatory
             NVQ standards in Care at Level 2   135
Appendix 4: Key legislation   136
Further reading   137
Sources of further information   139
About Age Concern   143
Publications from Age Concern Books   144
Index   149

About the author

Helen Howard has a varied career working freelance in a range of capacities including author of open learning materials, learning and development consultant and teacher in higher education. Her consultancy work covers everything from practice and procedure development for local authorities or the voluntary sector, to an audit of day care services for children in Romania.

Helen has set up and taught management and staff development programmes for local authorities and the voluntary sector. She also teaches *Understanding Health and Social Care* and *The Capable Manager* for the Open University and an MA in Community Development for the University of Kent at Canterbury.

Previous employment experience includes school teacher, adult education tutor, project manager, various posts with Kent Social Services and County Organiser for the Preschool Learning Alliance. Helen also chairs the Board of Directors of Canterbury Cyrenians, an organisation which provides accommodation and resettlement services for single homeless people.

Acknowledgements

Many people living and working in residential and nursing homes contributed to this book. Particular thanks are also due to the following care homes which made me welcome and answered my questions:

Barham House Nursing Home
Bossington Hall dual registered Nursing Home
Ennerdale Residential Care Home
Emily Jackson Nursing Home
Hamilton's Residential Care Home
Ladesfield Linked Service Centre
Littlebourne House Residential Care Home
Old Rectory, Ickham, Residential Care Home
Pinehurst Nursing Home
The New Close, Residential Care Home
West Kent Housing Association, Sheltered Housing With Special Care

I would also like to thank the following individuals and organisations:

Michelle Ashton, Care Sector Project, Canterbury Christ Church University College.
Karen Smith, University of Kent, for information on her research project.
Kent Inspection and Registration Unit for advice and guidance on the principles of care.
Paul Absolon for reviewing the manuscript.
Kent County Council Social Services Department for permission to use material from *Good Care: A guide to the good care of older people in residential care homes*; and *A Guide To Working With Older People With Mental Health Difficulties*.
Andy Davies and Canterbury College for reference material on the NVQ Standards in Health and Social Care.

Helen Howard

Introduction

Who this book is for

Most of us, as we get older, want to live in our own homes for as long as possible. The National Health Service and Community Care Act 1990 and the Government's policy paper *Modernising Social Services* stressed how important it was that we should be able to do so, if we wanted to. Eventually, for some people, however, there comes a time when illness, disability or frailty make it difficult to continue being cared for at home. When this happens, more specialist or more regular care may be needed 24-hours a day. This book is particularly for people who work in the residential and nursing homes which provide this kind of care.

Language is a powerful medium and the words we use to describe people are important. People who live in residential care and nursing homes may be referred to as 'patients', 'residents', 'clients', 'customers', 'citizens', 'consumers' or 'tenants' depending on the circumstances. To achieve a consistent style the word 'resident' will be used throughout this book.

Job titles vary from one care home to another. You might be called a 'careworker', 'keyworker' or 'carer', but we will use the term 'care assistant' throughout this book to avoid confusion.

Caring for people

Caring for people is a complex job involving a variety of:

- skills;
- abilities;
- attitudes; *and*
- knowledge.

It is essentially a practical activity which means that knowing about the role in theory is not enough. You need to be able to apply what you know to real situations.

Knowing what to do in any particular situation is not something that is easily taught: it takes time and experience. To be a good care assistant you have to be able to apply what you have learnt from books or from lessons in college or school or from your own life experience. Learning to think about what you are doing and how you do it are among the first steps to developing better care practice.

How this book can help you

Care work is often seen as a job that anyone can do and the important skills needed for the job are not widely recognised. It is particularly seen as a job for women who have learnt how to care for others through their life experience although men sometimes take up caring too. Care work tends to be low paid and many staff get very little training in how to do their job well.

This book is designed to give you a firm foundation of understanding on which to build. It sets out: the principles of good quality care in a residential or nursing home; and the knowledge and skills required to look after older people living away from their own homes.

Imagine that you are the manager of a residential home for older people. One of your care assistants is moving away from the area so you need to recruit someone new to take her place. What sort of skills and abilities do you think you would look for?

Maybe you thought of all or some of the following:

- enjoys the company of older people
- understands the process of ageing and wants to learn more
- has a caring attitude and is good with people
- takes a professional and responsible attitude towards work
- can follow instructions and fit into a team
- can identify problems and find solutions
- can produce well-written or spoken reports, care plans etc

We will look at the skills and abilities which care assistants need and how you can develop them.

This book will help you to carry out your current job to the best of your ability. It provides information about how to have your competence recognised through the system of National Vocational Qualifications (NVQs) or SVQs in Scotland. There is also guidance on other kinds of training available to help you achieve your career ambitions.

1 Setting the Scene

In this chapter we will look at the context of care today. We particularly examine:

- *Ageism and understanding ageing*
- *Care work is changing*
- *Care homes are all different*
- *Who pays for care*
- *The value base of care*

Ageism and understanding ageing

We are constantly being told that we live in an ageing society and many of us fear getting old and so frail that we are unable to care for ourselves. Living in residential and nursing care is not inevitable for all of us, however. How many older people do you think live in residential or nursing care?

Looking at figures published in *Social Trends*, we get an interesting picture of who lives in residential and nursing care. When we look at 1996, we find that, for people between the ages of 65 and 74, about 99 per cent were still able to continue living in their own homes.

If you live beyond the age of 80 then you are more likely to require residential or nursing care but the majority of people can still continue to live at home. For people who lived beyond the age of 85, in 1996, about 26 per cent required care away from their own homes. Most of us can thus probably expect to be able to continue living in our own homes throughout our lives.

The proportion of people in the population over the age of 50 has increased enormously over the last 50 years or so. A child who is born in the UK this year can expect to live much longer than a child who was born 30 or 40 years ago, because of improved health care and living conditions. Life expectancy now is much greater than it was and it has become more difficult to define old age. Retirement used to be a recognisable cut-off point but now that has become more flexible. Someone retiring from work at 60 or 65 may have another 20 years or more of active life ahead of them. Describing someone as old may not be helpful at all because it assumes that this group of people has something in common. It may be more helpful to look at the social process of ageing itself and try to understand that each of us responds differently to it.

It is all too easy to make assumptions about people based on stereotypes. We sometimes hear sweeping statements about groups of people such as:

'Young people nowadays don't want to work'

'Life begins at 40'

'Old people don't like showers, they prefer baths'

These statements are based on stereotypes which are not helpful. Ageism is about stereotyping older people. It can lead us to ignore the differences between people. Older people are all different just as younger people are too.

The whole of life is a continuous process of change and development which is sometimes referred to as the life cycle. Our progress through life has phases. Think for a moment about the phases your life has gone through.

Your own particular picture will be different from anyone else's but perhaps you can identify some of the following:

- Birth
- Growing up
- Schooldays
- Being a teenager
- Perhaps studying after leaving school

- Forming relationships, perhaps marriage
- Having children
- Finding work roles
- Caring for children and/or ageing relatives
- Retirement

If you talk to other people you will find that some of your life experiences will be similar to those of other people of your own age and others will be different.

Ageing often involves loss. People begin to lose their former social roles as they age. For example, they may no longer be identified by the job they did in the past and with that comes loss of status as well as loss of income. As their own parents die they are no longer seen as daughters and sons. But they may take on new roles such as grandparent or great aunt.

Retirement usually includes a loss of income which changes the balance of power within families and with the outside world. The things which older people have to give, such as time and experience, are less highly valued. Some older people continue to want the same level of active social life that they did when they were younger. But others prefer to gradually become less involved and seem content to 'watch the world go by'. However physical activity remains an important factor in maintaining health.

People's experience of getting older will depend on their income because this is closely linked to lifestyle. It will also be different for men and women. Women are often more vulnerable because they tend to live longer and are likely to have a lower income. People from black and other minority ethnic groups who have grown older in the UK may still feel like outsiders and will probably have difficulty in getting access to appropriate services because of discrimination.

The experience of ageing is unique for each person. Whatever their lives look like to other people, the important thing is how they feel about it themselves. The people who are most likely to experience ageing positively are those who feel they have at least some control over what is happening to them.

Care work is changing

People are able to stay in their own homes for much longer now than they could in the past. At one time, someone who was finding it difficult to look after themselves or was lonely following a bereavement, could choose to go into a care home and expect the State to pay the costs. This is no longer the case. Before someone can have their care home fees paid by the State, they have to be assessed as requiring care. Most people will also have to contribute towards the cost of their care according to their means. As a result of these changes, people who live in residential and nursing homes are likely to need more intensive care than in the past. So the role and responsibilities of careworkers have changed. Ideas about health and social care are changing all the time. Each year, new treatments are developed and new equipment is produced to assist older people with living as normal a life as possible. Here are the views of two experienced care staff:

Barbara, senior care assistant, nursing home

I've been working in care for 16 years and the equipment we use has changed a lot in that time. It was lifting all the time then. Now it's rules and regulations but we have hoists and all sorts. We have a lot of teaching sessions about the equipment so we know how to use it properly. We had a demo last week from someone at the local hospital. People come out of hospital quicker than they did in the past but I don't think the level of care has changed a lot in nursing homes in that time.

Ros, team leader, residential home

I've worked in care for 25–30 years now and the type of client we have has changed a lot. People are a lot more dependent than they used to be. They used to come in if they were lonely and wanted a social life. Now they are more physically frail. At the moment, I'd say we only have two who could probably manage on their own if they wanted to. One man is 99 and goes down the shops every day but he's been here 10 years since his wife died. He got really down and out then but he picked up really well in here.

These two examples suggest that:

- People moving into residential care now are likely to be more frail than they would have been in the past.
- Care work in a nursing home has not changed as much as care work in a residential home.
- New equipment, for example for lifting, may be making some aspects of care easier from the physical point of view.

Imagine yourself having to leave your own home with all its memories and the privacy and independence it provides. It must be a very difficult thing to do. As a care assistant you have to be sensitive to the needs of people living away from their own homes. Care work always was skilled, but it is even more important now for you to understand ageing and carry on learning new care skills throughout your career.

Care homes are all different

At April 1999 there were 554,100 places in residential settings for the long-stay care of older people and people with physical disabilities in the UK. Of those, 450,000 were in the private or voluntary sector. These figures do not include places in small homes with fewer than four beds (Laing and Buisson 1999).

Each residential or nursing home is unique. Let's look at the experience of two care assistants comparing the different places they have worked:

Sharma, care assistant, residential home

In a small home the whole routine is different. We don't wake people, they wake naturally. Some people just have breakfast when they want and go at their own pace. Some of the residents like to sit and peel vegetables in the kitchen like you would in a family. If something doesn't get done then the next shift will do it. In some of the big places I've worked it seemed like the people had to be managed like clockwork and fit into the routines of the home. It was like they didn't know how else to manage so many people. We didn't get a chance to get to know the residents because we were always in a hurry and we saw different faces every day.

Lynthia, senior carer, nursing home

It's less hands on in residential and I like the hands on so I prefer working in a nursing home. We try to get them to do as much as possible for themselves but we have to do more for them here than we did in the residential home I was at before. In residential work we had to do a lot of cleaning as well because people looked after themselves more.

These two workers have described some contrasts in the different kinds of care homes they have worked in and the different expectations of the way they had to work. The number and variety of choice of home has increased enormously over the last two decades. Homes may be run by:

- local authorities
- family businesses
- individuals
- housing associations
- trusts
- voluntary organisations
- large corporations

The kind of services the home provides to older people may be:

- specialist – for one particular type of illness or disability
- general to all frail older people
- nursing or residential only or dual registered for both types of care
- nursing care for younger disabled people as well as older people

Although care homes are all different there are some features which they have in common. We could say:

> 'A care home is a place where accommodation, food and care services are provided to people whose care needs cannot be met in their own home.' (Source: Residential Forum 1997)

Residents in a care home have:

- a right to occupy a specified room or rooms in a building which also contains some shared areas;
- a right to services provided by the owner of the building; *and*
- no direct employment relationship with the care staff.

They may have moved to the care home because they have become vulnerable in some way which makes it difficult for them to care for themselves at home.

The regulatory legislation makes a distinction between homes providing different kinds of care:

Residential homes provide care equivalent to that given by a competent relative. They do not have to employ qualified nurses.

Nursing homes provide nursing care by qualified nursing and auxiliary staff. They must have at least one qualified nurse on duty 24 hours a day.

Dual registered homes provide both residential and nursing care under the same roof, but they must have at least one qualified nurse on duty 24 hours a day.

The Care Standards Bill, which at the time of writing is not yet law, is expected to change the responsibilities for regulation but at the moment residential homes are registered by the local authority and nursing homes are registered by the health authority. Residential homes for four or more residents and all nursing homes are inspected at least twice a year. Residential homes for less than four people are registered but not currently required to be inspected although some local authorities do inspect them.

Older people may also live in sheltered accommodation where there is a warden available to provide assistance in an emergency. They may buy their flat or be a tenant but any care help they need is provided as though they were living in their own home. Some sheltered housing schemes provide extra care. Sheltered accommodation is not regulated under the Registered Homes Act 1984. Care is provided under a contract between each resident and a home care service, but sometimes this is a triangular relationship because the social services department pay for the care.

Who pays for care?

When someone needs more care than they can get in their own home then they may have to make the difficult decision to move into a care home. Care professionals are usually involved in helping to make the decision by carrying out an assessment of care needs. If someone has been assessed as requiring residential or nursing care, and needs help with funding, a financial assessment is carried out by the local authority social services department. Both income and capital are taken into account in this means test. Income includes all the regular payments which someone receives such as pension and most social security benefits. Capital includes savings, the value of any property the person owns (unless it is disregarded under the rules) and the value of their investments.

The calculation of how much the person will have to contribute towards their care depends on the rules at the time. In some homes the fee pays for all services provided, whereas in other homes there could be additional payments for such things as:

- newspapers
- laundry
- chiropody
- hairdressing
- incontinence pads

Every resident should have a personal allowance and be able to make choices about how to spend it. It is not acceptable for a home to take control of the way a resident's personal allowance is spent by making unreasonably high additional charges.

It is possible for someone looking for a care home to look in another area, particularly if the person is moving to be near a relative. It is more difficult for relatives and friends to visit residents if they are a long way away and particularly if travelling is a problem. If financial support is necessary then the prospective resident should be allowed to choose the home and location. In some cases, however, the local authority from where the resident comes will only pay the level of fees it would pay in its local area rather than the area to which the resident plans to move.

If someone is in hospital and has been assessed as requiring residential or nursing care, then their discharge from hospital is likely be arranged jointly. The people involved would probably be from the local authority social services department and the NHS professionals such as doctors, nurses and occupational therapists. Some people will go into long-term care which is also called continuing care and is paid for by the NHS. People who need continuing care may be looked after in a community hospital or a nursing home depending on the local arrangements.

If someone has to pay for the whole cost of their care then they may decide to arrange their own care without involving social services departments but it can be useful to have an assessment of needs to check out all the options.

The value base of care

Although we might disagree about some aspects of good quality care, there are some principles of good practice which most people would agree about:

- respecting dignity and privacy
- encouraging independence
- valuing individuality and difference
- promoting choice and self-esteem
- recognising rights and responsibilities
- maintaining a balance between safety and risk

We will look at each of these in more detail in this book.

Values are central to care work. They are what makes the difference in any kind of work with people. The importance of the value base of care is emphasised in all forms of training and education for people who work in health and social care. The Joint Awarding Body, which is responsible for developing Vocational Qualifications in Care, identified a set of values which should underpin good care practice:

- enabling people to develop to their full potential
- enabling people to communicate
- respecting individual beliefs and preferences
- promoting and supporting rights
- respecting privacy and confidentiality

Whether you want to get a Vocational Qualification or not, reading this book will help you to understand the value base of care.

KEY POINTS

- We are living in an ageing society.
- Ageing is different for each person but often involves loss. Ageist stereotypes are not helpful.
- It is important for older people to be able to live in their own homes for as long as they can.
- A care home is a place where accommodation, food and care services are provided to people whose care needs cannot be met in their own home.
- Care homes are regulated.
- Care is often provided under contract to local authorities but people may have to pay for their care, depending on their means.
- Ideas about health and social care, and therefore the role and responsibilities of care assistants, are changing all the time.
- Care work is a complex skilled job and it is important to carry on learning throughout your career.
- National Vocational Qualifications provide a framework for recognition of your skills.
- Good quality care has a value base and operates to a set of principles.

2 Being New

In this chapter we will look at starting a new job and make links between how it feels to be new in a job and how residents might feel about moving into a new home. We will look at:

- *Choosing where to work*
- *Going for an interview*
- *Your first day*
- *Induction and getting started*
- *How residents choose a care home*
- *Settling in for you and for new residents*
- *Getting to know the residents*

Choosing where to work

When you are choosing somewhere to work it is sensible to find out as much as you can about each care home. The philosophy of care is as important as how much you will be paid or the hours you will be expected to work. Each care home is a unique combination of its buildings, staff and philosophy of care.

Phil tells us about his experience of buying a nursing home and how he has tried to change it since he moved in:

Phil, owner of a nursing home

We bought this nursing home two years ago and we live here on the top floor: my mum, my wife and the children. It's a big old house set in its own gardens in a village street. We've got two small children so it helps living on site. We've got 20 residents which is small for a nursing home but this is our career; we're both nurses and we don't expect to make our fortunes.

We've made a lot of changes in two years. Some of the staff are the same people but I think they are less entrenched in routine than they were and the care assistants are more involved in evaluating care than they used to be. The trained nurses used to evaluate the care progress but now they are able to concentrate on drawing up and reviewing care plans and of course they countersign everything for the purposes of accountability. But to me it makes more sense that the care assistants evaluate progress and keep the care plans because they are the people who are most involved with the residents on a day to day basis. The first thing I did when I took over was throw away the bowel and bath books. At first the staff were aghast but I said to them: "If you want to know whether someone wants a bath, ask them." That seemed to be quite a novel idea!

Phil's example shows us the importance of the owner's philosophy of care. He wants the home run in a particular way which is different from the way it used to be run. The changes he wanted to make included:

- less routine;
- care assistants evaluating care plans (see pp 51-53 for more on care plans); *and*
- increasing residents' choice, for example over when they have a bath.

When unemployment is high and jobs are hard to come by, you may be tempted to take any work that is offered to you. Yet, as you can see from this case example, your role as care assistant may be very different depending on where you work. You need to be sure that you find a workplace that is right for you. The way you do this could be similar to the way residents choose a home.

When you are applying for work you should be provided with information about the home and asked to complete an application form. What sort of information do you think you need at this stage?

Perhaps you thought of:

- where the home is and how easy it would be to travel to and from work by public transport
- how much you would get paid
- what it would feel like to work there
- whether you would have to work different shifts
- whether you would have to do cleaning as well as personal care

At this stage you could go and look at the outside of the home and ask people you know whether they have friends or relatives who live or work there. You would be able to see whether the home is close to a busy road or to shops and community centres. You might see relatives, friends and residents going in and out of the home. On the other hand you might notice that the outside door is kept locked and want to know whether this restricts free movement for residents. Perhaps you can see residents sitting in the garden or at a window watching the world go by; you might be able to tell whether they look happy and cared for.

The kind of information you should be provided with by a prospective employer may include:

- a job description – an outline of the duties and responsibilities which the job involves (an example is given on pp 121–122);
- a person specification – the knowledge, skills and experience which the home is looking for;
- a copy of an up-to-date brochure showing the services which the home offers to residents; *and*
- the level of salary and also information about holiday entitlement and any benefits (for more details of your employee rights see Chapter 13).

Homes should also have handbooks for staff setting out their policies and procedures. A guide to the kind of things which may be included is provided in Appendix 1 on page 132.

Going for an interview

The application form should ask for sufficient information to enable the manager to make an initial judgement about your suitability for the post. You should be interviewed and asked to provide references from people who know you well, including previous employers or your school or college. Under the Rehabilitation of Offenders Act 1974 you will have to declare any convictions, including spent convictions, as part of your application. The police authority may then be asked to carry out a check to make sure that you are a safe person to work in a care home.

When you go for an interview you should get a chance to have a good look round. Most people get nervous when they are interviewed for a job. The sort of things which most people think about are: how to create a good impression; and how to give information about yourself to show that you can do the job.

You might like to make a list of the things you want to find out as well. What sort of things do you think you might want to know when you visit the home for an interview for a job?

The kind of questions you might want to think about include:

- how clean the home looks and smells when you first go in and on closer inspection
- whether residents look well-dressed, happy and cared for
- the number of ancillary staff there are – that is staff who do things like cooking and cleaning, gardening or driving the minibus
- initial impressions of the philosophy of care, such as how people talk to each other and the general atmosphere – is it rushed or relaxed, are relationships cool and clinical or warm and friendly?
- the level of care the residents receive – are they quite independent or do they need a lot of help? How alert are the residents to what is going on around them and are they talking to each other?
- the way staff ensure that the privacy and dignity of residents is maintained
- the ethnic mix of staff and residents and how the home accommodates differences, for example in religious customs and practice

- how much choice residents have in their lifestyles, such as on diet and food preferences, the times they get up and go to bed or how they spend their days
- the level of staff turnover – if staff change frequently there is probably something wrong. On the other hand if staff remain a long time you might want to know how they keep up to date and continue to learn new ways of working

In particular you will want to know how the philosophy and practice of the home is reflected in the work you will be expected to do.

Some homes employ activities organisers to work in various ways with residents during part of the day. In other homes care assistants are involved in organising activities such as painting, gardening or outings. Some homes employ cleaning and catering staff so that care assistants would be involved in direct work with residents for the whole of their shift. In other homes the care staff do the laundry and clean the bathrooms and bedrooms after they have helped residents to get up in the morning. So your role could be very routine and the same each day or it could be more varied and interesting depending on how the work is divided up between staff.

Turning down a job when you have been offered it may be a hard thing to do especially if you are on benefit or have very little work experience. But working in a home where the quality of care is poor and residents and staff are not treated well, can be soul-destroying.

Frances tells us something about the way she chose the care home where she wanted to work:

Frances, care assistant, residential home

I wanted to work here because one of my friends told me it was a good place. I worked nights in another place before I came and the people there weren't treated as good as they are here. When I used to help people dress in that other place some of them still had the clothes on that I'd put on them two days before. Here everybody changes all their clothes every day. Their clothes are kept nice which is about their dignity isn't it? The bed linen is good quality too so the sheets feel nice to touch.

Frances is happy in her present choice of job but having had some unpleasant experiences of care work in the past she had learnt the hard way that care work is different in different homes.

Your first day

Starting a new job is never easy, although Frances, from our previous case example, thinks that she is the only one who gets nervous on the first day:

Frances, care assistant, residential home

I've always worked with old people – I like them. I work in the community too which is nice – I get a bit of variety. It's for the same company so I can work my hours in. The community work is helping with shopping and domestic work, that kind of thing.

Although I had done a lot of care work, the first day I started here I was really apprehensive, but I think that's just me. It's difficult to go into a new situation where you don't know anyone. But the staff were very helpful. They're a nice group. It was such a new experience working with a group of staff as a team. I hadn't worked in a home like this before. But the others took me through the routine and showed me what to do. Before it was like being my own boss. Although I had a boss he wasn't standing over me all the time telling me what to do. I had to use my own initiative and make it up as I went along really. I've only been working here three months. They have a three day induction programme about the company and all the rules and regulations but I've been here three months and I haven't been on it yet.

When you come for interview and they tell you about the work there are things they don't tell you. What I wasn't expecting was for people to just go to the toilet wherever they wanted. It's like they have reverted to childhood habits. It's obvious if you think about it I suppose, but it was a shock. There are other things they do which I don't think I can talk about.

We can see from Frances' story that even someone who had a lot of work experience caring for older people still found it difficult to adjust to working in a care home rather than as a home help in the community. She was also taken by surprise by the level of care which the residents needed in this particular home. Her first day was made easier for her because the staff group was welcoming and helpful.

Induction and getting started

Frances mentioned induction, which is the early training which a new member of staff needs to get used to a new job. Let's look at some examples of how this is organised:

Sonia, senior nurse, dual registered home

When someone new starts I explain to them what the role of the care assistant is. I say it is to look after the residents who live here and make it as safe and comfortable as possible for them. We try not to have too many rules and regulations, though with 36 people you have to have some. So we try to make it as much like home as possible.

Induction lasts a month. I always say we don't expect people to be perfect all at once. There's always someone they can ask if they are not sure what to do.

Ros, team leader, residential home

Induction time is a time for individual attention and that works quite well. You explain all the policies and procedures when they first start and identify their training needs before they go on the shop floor. We don't let them near the residents on their own until we are sure they know what they are doing. We can't let them find out by trial and error. It's not fair on the residents.

Raoul, team leader, residential home

When people come for interview I give everybody a list of what they would have to do each day. Then there aren't any surprises if they get the job. Induction lasts a month. It starts with them shadowing me for a week and a half and I explain what I am doing as I go. Then we change over so I'm shadowing them for another week and a half. After that I give them feedback on how they are doing and ask them how they think they are doing. I ask them what they think about the way we do things and try to make it a two-way thing. At the end of the month if they fit in we ask them to sign a contract. After that they have to give us a month's notice if they want to leave. That gives us some time to fill their place. If they turn out not to be suitable we can ask them to leave straightaway during that month.

For the first year the training they get is all provided in-house, so we show them how to use the lifting equipment and how to keep records, using the computer, what to do in emergencies and all those sorts of things. Then I've written a little exam which I give them after six months. It just asks questions about all the things they've learnt, the care routines or health and safety, like: how can you preserve someone's privacy and dignity while you are helping them to get dry after having a bath? Or: which days are there teatime discussion groups? Because it's part of a keyworker's job to tell their client what's happening in the home and encourage and support them to join in if they want to. We have quite a few staff who have been with us for more than a year and they then go on to college courses and we can assess them for NVQs. We use a lot of the courses run by the Health Promotion Unit on things like continence.

As you can see from these examples, induction varies from one care home to another. Perhaps you might want to ask questions about induction when you go for interview to find out what the arrangements are in that particular care home. The kind of things you might expect induction in your first few days to include are:

- daily tasks
- philosophy of care
- basic health and safety

This should then be followed up with a more in-depth training programme.

How residents choose a care home

Now we've looked at how you would go about choosing where to work, let's think a bit more about the way residents go about the difficult business of deciding where to spend the rest of their lives. If you were trying to find a care home for yourself or for a relative, what would you look for?

Iris is 84 and needs support 24 hours a day since she had a stroke:

Iris, resident in a care home in a busy seaside town

I liked Woodside as soon as I saw it because everyone was smiling and seemed to be enjoying themselves. When I came to look round, the minibus had just come back from an outing with the Bowls Club. I used to enjoy bowling before I had my stroke – there's a lot of skill in it you know and I won the trophy two years running. I can't play any more of course but I still like watching it and just being with the Club too. We used to have a few laughs in those days. We are really near the sea here too so I can take a turn along the promenade when the weather's fine and see all the amusement arcades and the funfair. Or just sit on the verandah and watch the waves, the ferries going in and out or the people walking by in the rain. You see some funny sights! There's always something happening here.

Iris made the choice which was right for her. She liked being with other people and with lots of noisy things happening, but perhaps you would want peace and quiet or a small home with few residents where everyone organises their own lives. Other people might be looking for closeness to shops and busy community centres or a large home where group activities are organised every day.

Muriel wanted somewhere quiet:

Muriel, resident in a care home in a quiet village

I love the garden. It is gorgeous: going right down to the river, with a big summer house that you can open right up and nice wooden chairs. I spend a lot of time out there. I've kept a diary since I moved in: I watch the birds and write down everything I see. There was a kingfisher last week. The men cut back the trees so the kingfisher can fly right down to the bridge. I've seen a heron twice too. But I was worried about there being so few insects this year. There isn't anything for the birds to eat.

The main point we might draw from these examples is that different people will look for different things when they choose a care home. Most people begin with a list of names and addresses and phone numbers. Just think for a moment: if you were given a list of 20 or 30 care homes in your area, what would you do to try and find out which one might provide what you want?

Perhaps you thought of:

- asking each one for a copy of their brochure
- talking to friends to find out if anyone you know has visited any of them
- looking at the map to see where they are in relation to public transport and shops or community centres
- making an appointment to visit a few

Let's look at some more examples:

Iris, resident

I got my daughter to take me out on a visit to four of the homes on my list before I chose this one. When you read the brochures it's a bit like reading stuff in adverts in an estate agent's window or holiday brochures. Some of them look alright but you don't know what they are really like until you live there.

Joan, daughter of a resident

When we came back from holiday Mum had had another fall. Fortunately my sister-in-law had called round and got the doctor. Mum talked to the social worker and district nurse about whether she could carry on at home and decided to have a look at a few places just to see what they were like really. When we got to The Lodge Mum found there were two people living there that she knew from way back. One chap she went to school with and hadn't seen for about 50 years. Anyway, to cut a long story short, she decided to go there which was quite a relief for me because although I don't mind keeping an eye out for her I can't be there all the time and she had fallen quite a few times before. It was meeting people she knew there that made the difference.

Before someone moves into a care home they should have been provided with information about a range of different homes so that they can make a choice. This may have included visiting several to see what they are like and talking to managers, staff and other residents to find out about the way of life in the home. A trial period of stay of a few days or weeks may then be arranged. So, as care assistant, you may first meet a resident during their trial period before they have decided whether or not to stay.

Settling in for you and for new residents

Moving house can be as difficult to deal with as a death in the family. Leaving your own home and moving into a care home can be an emotional experience involving all kinds of feelings, including:

- loss and separation
- rejection
- helplessness
- apathy
- anger

If you have lived in the same house for many years it will have many associations with the past. Perhaps other people have lived there too: friends, partners, parents or children. A house is also associated with a neighbourhood, with familiar streets and familiar faces. The change can renew old feelings of loss and separation from loved ones and generate new grief.

> **Marjorie, resident, residential home**
>
> My first day here was three years ago when the home first opened. It was a very emotional day for me because I was leaving my own home and Chris (staff) was new too. There was just the two of us then. So we spent the day talking to each other and getting to know each other. It was emotional for both of us I think and then the others started coming in one by one and gradually things changed. But there's always been this special thing between Chris and me because we were new together and I was the first.

As a care assistant you need to be aware of the way a new resident might be feeling and do all you can to help them. Let's have a look at another case example:

Kim, team leader, residential home

If we can arrange a planned admission, people start by coming to the day centre and for the occasional respite week or two. If they've been in here on respite it's quite nice because they know us. We always try to give new residents an introductory couple of hours in the day centre if we can. But sometimes people come in as an emergency straight from hospital and we can't do much about that. It's much more difficult to settle people then.

Some people come in for two weeks and go home for two weeks regularly because that's all their carer can take. We get used to working with people but it must get on your nerves living with someone who is in a bad way 24 hours a day. One of the things we have to deal with all the time is relatives' guilt. They feel bad about not looking after their parents and that makes them quite demanding on us. If they are checking up on us, it kind of makes up for their not doing the caring themselves. I don't think they should feel bad about it. Caring for someone who has dementia is hard and I need my time off. If you are living with it you don't get any time off and that must be awful.

The main points Kim makes are:

- Planned admissions are easier for residents.
- It is important for care assistants to be aware of relatives' feelings too.

For the resident it must be hard to admit that you can't cope on your own any more. Someone who has been looked after by friends or relatives immediately before moving into a care home, may feel rejection when those people can no longer cope. Even if the decision is perfectly reasonable, there will still be feelings to deal with. As a care assistant you may notice that someone new is upset. They may show anger or they can become listless and find it difficult to join in. It is important to realise that these feelings may not be caused by something you have done, although you may be on the receiving end.

Adjustment to the new situation takes time but will be affected by the way people are treated. Each person will react to it differently and for some the change may be very welcome if they have been struggling to manage alone. The first few weeks of adjustment set the pattern for the future. This is the time when routines are established and people get used to each other and to the way things are in the home. When residents are able to bring familiar possessions with them it helps to make the new place feel like home. Maintaining contact with former friends and family as well as the wider community that the resident belonged to may also help.

All homes have a set of informal rules and patterns of behaviour which newcomers may not at first notice. Anyone who has watched the behaviour of people on a beach will know that, just like other animals, we tend to be territorial. Existing residents in a care home may each have their own preferred chair, for example, so a newcomer will need to be guided in their choice of where to sit in communal areas. If the building is large it may be easy to get lost if you don't know your way around. Perhaps someone new can be 'shown the ropes' in the early days by an existing resident.

Getting to know the residents

New residents bring a history and a lifetime of experience with them which you can use to get to know them. We tend to identify ourselves by the roles we play, such as daughter, father, teacher, bus driver, husband or wife, care assistant. These roles are part of our identity: they are an important part of making us who we are and showing how we fit into the world. Older people tend to lose those roles through life-changing events such as bereavement and retirement. Someone who moves into a care home loses other kinds of roles, such as householder and neighbour.

Talking to someone new about their history, including the roles they have played in the past, helps you to get to know them as people and helps them to rebuild their identity and self-esteem.

In some homes reminiscence is used as a form of therapy for older people. Chris, who is head of care in the home where Marjorie lives, talks about reminiscence as part of her activity programme:

Chris, head of care, residential home

In the afternoons we do whatever we fancy together – quizzes or crosswords or just talking about the good old days. I've got a reminiscence book which jogs my memory about things like the old blue bag you used to put in the washing, ration books, the way they used to put your money into a canister on a railway above your head in some of the big shops and the smell of the medicine cupboard – the stink of embrocation for bruises and sore muscles. Talking is just a nice way to get to know each other.

If you are interested in reminiscence therapy you can read more about it in Age Concern's book *Reminiscence and Recall* (see p 144).

KEY POINTS

- Each care home is a unique combination of its premises, staffing and philosophy of care.
- When choosing where to work, the philosophy of care in the home is as important as how much you will be paid and the hours you will be expected to work.
- Your role as care assistant could be very routine and similar each day or it could be varied and interesting depending on where you work.
- Collect as much information as you can about a care home before deciding whether you want to work there.
- Find out about the induction programme for new staff.
- Moving house can be as difficult for residents to deal with as a death in the family. It creates similar feelings of loss. As a care assistant you have an important role in helping new residents to adjust.
- Relatives may feel guilty about not being able to provide care and they need your support too.
- Residents bring a history and lifetime of experience with them. Getting to know that history and the roles they have played helps them to rebuild their identity and self-esteem.

3 A Day in the Life of a Care Assistant

In this chapter we will look at what may be expected of you in your job including:

- *Establishing good relationships*
- *Communication skills*
- *Daily tasks*
- *Rotas, night work and shift patterns*
- *Keyworking*

Establishing good relationships

Care is a difficult word to define because it refers not only to something which people do for each other but also to the feelings that people have for each other. Receiving care is an experience which each resident will react to in their own individual way. This will depend partly on their previous experience. It will also depend on how they feel about what is happening to them and the way they see you and your role. Marjorie, who is a resident in a residential home, talks about how she feels about how she is cared for:

> **Marjorie, resident, residential home**
>
> Chris (head of care) is wonderful: they are so careful about how they select staff here, they only take the best. If you need help in going to the toilet or something, you only have to call and they are there. And the boys (the owners) are caring lads. When they are here they will often come in and say: "Anyone fancy a day out?

Where shall we go?" And we pile into the cars and off we go. It's always spontaneous and I like that. It must be awful to know it's Thursday so it must be bingo today. I like surprises. I don't think you could better this place. Where else would you get sweets on your pillow and a fruit bowl to help yourself whenever you want?

Marjorie is not talking here just about the care tasks which appear on someone's job description. When we think about care we need to remember that it is not only about physical care. It also has social, intellectual and emotional aspects to it. As a care assistant you need to meet:

physical needs – cleanliness, mobility etc
intellectual needs – activities which stimulate thought
emotional needs – love, loss, anger etc
social needs – relationships, belonging etc

Marjorie has referred to all of these in her description of the care she receives:

physical needs – such as help in going to the toilet, good food
intellectual needs – such as unexpected events
emotional needs – such as that she feels cared for; there is warmth in the way she speaks about the head of care and the owners
social needs – the care home is a place where she feels she belongs

Quality of care for Marjorie, and for most people, depends on establishing a good relationship with the person who is being cared for.

Communication skills

Communication is a word we use a lot and it is one of the key skills of care. We spend most of our lives communicating without even realising it. But what do you think communication means?

Lots of people only think of talking when they think about communication but it includes listening and writing too. You are communicating most of the time in lots of different ways. Perhaps you thought of some of the following:

- smiling at someone
- answering the telephone
- having a conversation with a friend
- responding to a question or something someone else has said
- listening when someone wants to talk
- comforting someone through touch when they are upset
- collecting and storing information to put into a report
- writing or reading a letter
- giving a talk
- selecting and recording relevant information by taking notes in a lecture or from reading a book
- using pictures or diagrams to illustrate an idea
- using a computer to write an essay
- discussing something important with work colleagues, by looking at all aspects of an issue and making a decision on what to do

Communication is an everyday activity with many aspects to it. Indeed all interactions are a means of communicating and it has a particularly important role in care work. Residents may have difficulty letting you know their needs, whether because of speech or language differences or loss of the ability to hear well, or because they are not used to expressing their views and wishes. Environmental factors such as lighting and noise levels can affect whether you can hear or be heard. As you have probably noticed from your own family experience, when music or the television is on, it becomes difficult to hold a conversation.

When someone is able to express their views, feelings and wishes clearly without being aggressive this is called being assertive. Being assertive will be very valuable for you in your role as care assistant. It is also something that residents may need to practice, because not everyone is used to expressing themselves clearly. If you can be assertive it will help those around you to behave in the same way.

Good communication is vital to building good relationships between you and the people you care for, as well as the other people you work with and meet every day. When you are a care assistant you bring your own personality with you to work and that affects how you do the job. This is what Cordalee has to say:

Cordalee, care assistant, nursing home

I love them all. Some are a bit scratchy but it's part of the job. I like the hands on nursing and I like to have time for them. I like to laugh and joke with them. Laughter is uplifting and healing. That's what I try to bring to my work. Then they are cheeky back to me. I sing a lot too and that's how they know where I am. I talk while I work. I really enjoy making a lovely bed for someone to get into. I think of it like it was my mother or father. They all have a life and a history and I never forget that.

The way we communicate with other people can convey trust and confidence and it strongly affects the way people feel about the care they receive. Warm feelings can be generated through the expression on your face and even the way you stand or walk. On the other hand if you are upset or angry people around you will soon know, as Eve explains:

Eve, care assistant, nursing home

I was really depressed one morning. My kids were playing up at home and it was raining so I couldn't put the washing out. But I didn't realise how much it showed until Mrs Snow asked me what was wrong. She asked me into the office and told me she could tell I was miserable because I wasn't smiling like I usually do and I was walking with my shoulders all hunched up. She persuaded me to talk things over and after a while I could see that my troubles weren't important enough to ruin every one else's day as well. It is quite difficult sometimes to put your life outside work on hold until the end of the shift but somehow you have to.

Interpersonal skills in a care setting also includes the way you touch people. Lots of care work includes touch, such as when you offer someone an arm for support as they walk along or help someone to dress or undress. Touching someone sends signals to them which may be misinterpreted because touch is often associated with sex. Older people who have lost their partners sometimes feel deprived of touch but it is not reasonable to assume that everyone wants to be touched. (Pages 42–43 give more information about touch.)

Daily tasks

Each care home will have its own patterns of working and will expect different things of its care assistants. Let's have a look at the experience of the following people who work in different care homes:

Barbara, senior care assistant on the morning shift, nursing home

Most days are the same but sometimes you get an odd one that's different. I work 7am till 12pm each morning so I help with the breakfasts when I come in. Some people like to eat their breakfast sitting up in bed but other people like to get up and sit in a chair. Then we help people to get up, have a bath if they want one and get dressed. We have half an hour to 40 minutes with each person so there is plenty of time to talk and help them to do things for themselves.

I've been working in care homes on and off for ten years now. When I came to work here the first time I had just left school and I thought all care homes were the same but they're not. I've worked in other places where you have to rush all the time because there aren't enough staff. You would sometimes only get quarter of an hour per patient and that's not long enough and they know you're rushing. But here it's different. The afternoon shifts are quieter. We tend to do baths in the morning and we ask who wants one. Some like one every day or every other day. One lady likes hers on a Thursday, so you get to know.

Most people are mobile and nobody is bedridden except temporarily when they are ill. If somebody's ill we make sure someone sits with them. We take everyone out if we can even if it's only into the garden. They go out for walks in the village too. We had a barbecue the other day for someone's birthday and another man wanted to go down the pub for his birthday so we did.

Sam, afternoon shift worker, in the same nursing home

I work afternoon shifts usually, that's 1pm till 8pm. When we come in at 1 o'clock we usually start by doing a toilet round. We toilet two hourly with the ones who are incontinent. After lunch we put some people to bed if they have been sitting all morning to relieve the pressure on their bottoms. They are on air mattresses to relieve the pressure. I worked in a hospital for a while and the patients were always getting pressure sores there because they didn't have the right mattresses. They don't get them here.

Usually we have some sort of activities in the afternoon. The nurse in charge and one of the carers do an exercise class. They have a sponge ball to throw and catch which makes them move about. You can have a real laugh with them when they go out of their way to catch it. There is a lady comes in to do painting too and bingo sometimes. We have the school readers too. They are children from the local primary school and they come in to read to the patients. There are some patients who always have them so they get to know each other.

We have tea at 3pm. There are visitors in all the time of course and their relatives often take them out. If it's hot we take people out into the garden and we all get involved in whatever is happening. The more you stimulate people the better.

Supper is at 5pm. Then we get them ready for bed before we go. Some people stay up: three or four stay up quite late. It's the patient's choice when they go to bed.

Yasmina, care assistant, nursing home, talking about the tasks at the end of a shift

It's near the end of my shift so I'm just writing up my end of shift reports. It's just a few lines about whether they have achieved their goals today like whether they were able to wash their hands themselves, their mood, if they've had any visitors, if the physio has been to see them or if they've eaten well. That sort of thing. When you come on shift you start off by reading the book. We don't have verbal handovers any more and this is much better because you don't have to listen to a lot of stuff about people you aren't looking after. You don't remember half of it anyway. This way it is there in the book so if you forget you can go back and read it again.

Sandra, manager, dual registered home

The morning shift here starts at 8am with the breakfast trays being collected. Some people like breakfast in bed but others like to have theirs sitting up in a chair. As soon as we've cleared up we all meet together in the hall to discuss any problems, talk about what's happened during the night and get people up to date if they've been off for a few days. We allocate work at that stage, deciding who is going to work where. We usually split the care staff into two groups each of three people and they work a floor together. They sort the work out between them to some extent because they get to know who is going to need a lot of help and who doesn't.

Then the groups go off and start getting people up and washed and dressed. Some will already be up and dressed of course. Others need a lot of help and some prefer to stay in bed. So some people need more than one person to move them about. We do baths, there's a bath rota, and hair washing, make up if they want it, check their skin and do dressings. This is always done under the supervision of the nurse on duty that day. That takes until about 11am.

11am is hot drink time for residents and staff. We have a team of domestic staff who do that and all the cleaning and laundry so the care staff don't do any cleaning. The domestics chat to the residents too. After that we do toileting and changing pads so that people are ready for lunch.

12.30pm to 1.30pm is lunchtime and everyone gathers together for that to make it a social occasion. There are two dining rooms and the care assistants help people to eat or cut their food up – whatever's required.

After lunch some people will want to go to the toilet again. Some then go to bed for a lie down, some doze in a chair.

We try to organise various activities in the afternoons. The care assistants might do craft work in the conservatory, chair exercises or play bingo with the residents. We have a minibus so we take them for a ride out if it's fine. Perhaps a wheelchair ride down the road to the farm. They can sit in the garden or knit. We have library books which the library changes every three months. Families take people on outings sometimes. Care staff also do people's nails and chat to them or help with letter writing.

Dr Bright comes once a week on a Thursday and holds a clinic, to see her patients or any that we are worried about. She would help us reassess patients if we think they should be receiving nursing care and not residential care because we take both here.

There's a tea break at 3pm then more toileting. Teatime is 5.30pm to 6.30pm and the shift changes during tea.

The evening shift runs from 6pm to 10.30pm and they get people ready for bed with some bathing and most people are in bed by the time the night shift come on.

The night shift runs from 10.30pm. Some people need changing or turning if they can't turn themselves and others will need a complete bed change. If someone doesn't settle in bed they can use a recliner chair instead. The night staff also do any laundry that needs putting on. That's a 24 hour a day job really. The machines are going continuously. The night staff give people their breakfasts before the day shift starts again at 8am.

Marian, senior care assistant, residential home

The day shift is from 8am to 8pm. The night shift usually give residents their breakfast in their rooms before we start. From 8am onwards we spend the next two hours helping people to get up and washed and dressed. Not everyone needs help of course. Some people like to have a bath at that time. Some people prefer the afternoons. They all have a bath at least once a week but they can ask for one any time they like. When they are up we make the beds and give each person a jug of fresh water or squash in their room.

They have coffee or tea at 10am and then we start laying the trays for lunch. There are two dining rooms so they can eat together if they want to but most people have lunch in their rooms. Three people usually eat together in the upstairs dining room and five in the downstairs one. Then they probably have a nap.

We do their washing during the day and the night shift do the ironing. So we take their clean clothes into them in the afternoon and stop for a chat. Supper is at 6pm but the times of meals aren't fixed: they can eat later if they want to. We get people ready for bed before we go off the shift at 8pm if they need help – then they can go to bed whenever they want.

You probably noticed that this group of care staff all have different things to tell us about the tasks which care assistants may be expected to do and how they might do them. Depending on which shift you are doing the tasks might include:

• helping residents to get up, washed and dressed
• preparing for mealtimes and clearing away afterwards

- talking to residents and keeping them informed about what is happening
- helping with activities and outings
- making sure that residents have drinks available in their rooms when they want them
- changing bed linen
- personal care, such as helping residents to go to the toilet or have a bath
- doing the laundry
- nursing care, such as changing dressings
- keeping written records, such as care plans
- communicating with other staff, for example through handover meetings or through a day book

There were quite a lot of differences between the work in different kinds of homes or on different shifts in the same home.

Rotas, night work and shift patterns

Most people living in residential or nursing care need staff to be present 24 hours a day and this is normally a regulatory requirement. But different numbers of staff are usually required at different times of the day; for example mornings and evenings are when residents are getting up or going to bed and so are often busier than other times of the day. This means that care staff often work hours which office staff would think were unusual.

Some homes recruit staff to work the same pattern of hours every week; for example they may advertise for someone to work mornings only. If you have childcare arrangements to make, it is helpful to be able to work the same hours each work. But many people are happy to vary their hours of work from week to week and may find it makes the job more interesting. It is often difficult for homes to find staff who are willing or able to work at night. Night work is a very different experience from daytime working. Let's look at Shirley's experience of night work:

Shirley, night care assistant, nursing home

The night shift here starts at 8pm with the trained nurse doing the drugs round. Then we do evening drinks and there will still be four or five who aren't in bed. They ring when they want help. We check everyone when we first come on duty. Some people need two hourly care through the night and there's one man who needs to go to the toilet several times. Sometimes we might have to change pads or change the bed.

We do the laundry on the night shift; washing, drying and folding. The ironing gets done at the weekend and then we put things away. So on the weekend night shift the laundry can take until 3am sometimes.

Then we tidy up the lounge and set the breakfast trays. I usually check my care plans when I come on night shift at the weekends so I am ready for the week.

We start doing rounds at 6am in case anyone is awake and breakfasts usually start about 7am. Sometimes we have pads and beds to change but I finish at 8am and the day staff take over and finish off whatever still needs to be done.

From Shirley's case you can see that the kind of work which night care staff do is quite different from the work of a care assistant in the daytime. Peter tells us something about the kind of situations which he sometimes has to deal with at night:

Peter, night care assistant, residential home

Night shift is different because you don't get to keywork. There are three staff on at night including a teamleader but there is a good call-out system for backup. We can call out the manager or assistant manager any time if we're worried about something. Our job then is to make sure people get a good night's sleep. We've only got three people who regularly take sleeping pills to help them sleep. The rest just sleep naturally and if they get up I can usually talk them into going back to bed. I was on nights last weekend and we've got a vicar who got up in the night because he thought he was going off to preach a sermon somewhere but I told him what time it was and said he still had time to get another forty winks before he had to go. So I suppose you bend the truth a bit sometimes. We've got another chap who used to be a poacher so he sometimes wants to sleep all day and get up in the night to catch rabbits. But I tell him I haven't seen any rabbits about so he might as well go back to bed. I tell him I'll let him know if I see any.

Sleep patterns may also become disrupted as we get older. The quality of sleep may decline because we sleep less deeply or for shorter periods. When there is very little happening during the day, older people may tend to dose through it and then feel less tired at bedtime than they would after an active stimulating day. A care home may seem noisy at night as each person goes to bed or gets up to go the toilet and staff cope with the laundry. Lights may also be left on for those who need to find their way to the bathroom and this can be distracting. Your role as care assistant if you are working the night shift is to do all you can to help residents get a good night's sleep. However, it is quite normal for older people to need less sleep and they should be allowed to manage their night-time lifestyle in their own way.

Looking at these case examples, we can assume that the care assistant's role on a night shift may include:

- helping residents get a good night's sleep
- visiting any residents who have agreed that this is necessary as part of their care plan
- making as little noise as possible
- avoiding switching on the lights as far as possible
- checking that each person is lying in a comfortable position
- turning people who are at risk of developing pressure sores
- making a note of any signs of illness or discomfort
- taking action if someone needs extra care

- washing and changing any residents who need it
- being prepared to talk quietly to people who want to talk and provide anything they need such as cups of tea to help them go back to sleep

Keyworking

Some homes have a keyworker scheme in place. This is a system where you would take particular responsibility for a small group of residents. You might, for example, be the person who:

- helps them to get up in the morning
- deals with physical needs such as bathing and shaving
- discusses and takes note of clothing needs
- helps with shopping
- meets and gets to know their relatives
- arranges appointments
- passes on information about events and activities
- arranges visits and outings
- provides a reminder about important dates like birthdays

You would probably get to know these few residents very well and be involved in making sure that they are receiving the care recommended in the care plan. You would probably be involved in reviewing their care plans too. Through the development of this kind of closer relationship you may help the residents to develop a greater sense of belonging. As someone is taking a particular interest in them, the residents will find it easier to maintain their sense of self-respect and individuality. It will probably also give you a greater sense of job satisfaction.

As keyworker, you would not, however, be the only one who provides care for this group of people. They should feel they can ask for help from any of the care staff in the home. Also, not least because of the shift system, there will be times when you are not there.

KEY POINTS

- Care is a difficult word to define because it refers not only to something which people do for each other but also to the feelings that people have for each other.
- Care involves meeting physical, intellectual, emotional and social needs.
- Communication skills are vitally important to quality care.
- Each care home has its own patterns of working and expects different things of its care assistants. There are quite a lot of differences between the work in different kinds of homes or on different shifts in the same home.
- A keyworker takes particular responsibility for a group of residents.

4 Respecting Privacy and Dignity

In this chapter we look at the principles of care in the area of respecting residents' privacy and dignity. In particular we examine:

- *Preserving dignity*
- *Touch and intimate care*
- *Personal and private space*
- *Death and dying*
- *Using preferred names*
- *Confidentiality and being discreet*
- *Personal relationships*
- *Personal belongings, hygiene and self-esteem*

Preserving dignity

Preserving the privacy and dignity of residents should be very important to all the staff who work in a care home. Our sense of identity comes from past experience, from such things as our race, gender, culture, religion or social class. It also comes from the way other people treat us in the present.

Each of us has personal habits which are peculiar to us and we wouldn't want the rest of the world to know about. Think for a moment about the things you do that might annoy other people. Maybe you snore or spend hours in the bathroom in the mornings when other people are waiting. Group living brings with it the fear that other people will find out about us, or that we will have to put up with other people's personal smells and eating habits. Nonetheless it is perfectly possible for people in a care home to maintain their dignity and privacy with the help of good care staff. This is how Kevin tries to achieve that in the way he works:

Kevin, team leader, residential home

I talk to the residents all the time while I'm working, explaining what I'm doing and persuading them to cooperate. You have to be sort of bright and cheerful with them but at the same time you mustn't be patronising, so it's like general conversation like you would to anyone else.

If someone with dementia is incontinent, you have to try and get them cleaned up to preserve their dignity but sometimes they don't want to cooperate. We never use force but if someone needs cleaning up, you have to somehow get people to do what you want. It is difficult for them to understand sometimes. They get agitated and abusive. I keep a respectful distance so they don't feel threatened by me and so that I don't get attacked. But you always have to remember that if they abuse you they've forgotten what they've done a few minutes later. So when you have left them for a few moments to cool off you can go back in as though nothing had happened. And they'll say "Hello sonny, how are you?", as though they were greeting you for the first time that day. I always tell them my name, but they don't remember it and I don't think most of the residents know who I am. They think I'm their son or brother probably.

I've got one man I keywork for who I've been looking after for four years now. You get to know someone well in that time – he used to be a teacher. Some of the staff here knew him when he was a respected member of village life. He used to write books and Joanne said she's got some of his books. It's difficult to believe he's the same person sometimes when he is shuffling about here. He seems to have forgotten all the social norms like where it is appropriate to go to the toilet. I got to know his wife too and I talk to her about his progress. We have six-monthly reviews with the family and his care manager, when we talk about the changes that have happened. Like he has fits and I might say: "Well he had one grand mal on the 12th July but the one before that was way back in April, so that's good." He's taking his medication and most of the time he's okay. But of course I've seen him get worse in that time. I've kept his care plans all that time so I can look back and see what's happened.

As you can see from this account, Kevin does everything he can to preserve the residents' dignity in some very difficult circumstances. The important factors seem to be that he:

- sees the residents as individuals;
- talks to the residents, explaining what he is doing all the time;
- never uses force;
- keeps cheerful but respectful in his manner; *and*
- remembers that aggression is soon forgotten.

Touch and intimate care

Personal care inevitably involves touch and particularly touching areas of someone else's body which you would not normally touch. Society has unwritten rules about touch. Think for a moment about what you think these rules are.

Perhaps you thought about some or all of the following:

- patting someone on the head or shoulder as a sign of authority
- women may be more likely to touch one another than men
- touch often has a sexual meaning
- sometimes it causes embarrassment
- touch is associated with parents and babies but the rules on touching change as children grow up
- the rules of touch are different in different cultures (see Chapter 6)

Being naked when the other person in the room is fully clothed can involve embarrassment and the naked person will probably feel very vulnerable. One of the ways medical staff deal with this is to keep as much of their patient covered as possible. For example, if a nurse is giving someone a bed bath she will only uncover one section of the patient's body at a time. Towels and dressing gowns can be used in a similar way in a bathroom or when you are helping someone to wash and get dressed in the morning.

One of the things which nurses learn as part of their training is how to manage embarrassment. Generally speaking, if you are able to appear unembarrassed then the resident is less likely to be embarrassed too. This is about managing your reactions and responses to people rather than your feelings. As a care assistant you will learn how to deal with nakedness and touch in a way which minimises embarrassment on both sides and is acceptable to the residents.

Personal and private space

You may have noticed when someone you are talking to is standing too close for comfort, perhaps because they are short-sighted. This feeling of discomfort is because they are invading that area around you which we call 'personal space'. If you have ever travelled on public transport in the rush hour you will know how difficult it can be in some circumstances to protect your personal space, particularly when you are facing the other passengers. Personal space is linked with privacy and the way we deal with this kind of invasion may be to gaze ahead of us, perhaps look at the floor or at the advertisements above everyone's heads. We might want to compare this with the situation where residents in a care home may sit in the same room without speaking to each other. In that situation each person has created their own private space around them. It may be the only way to have privacy in a communal area.

Where a care home has single bedrooms and perhaps en suite bathrooms, each person has their own territory where they can keep their own habits private. Shared bedrooms usually mean loss of privacy. If someone comes into the care home from hospital then they may have become accustomed to sharing a large ward and find sharing with one other person preferable. For most people, however, sharing rooms can be a difficult adjustment and it is becoming less common as general housing standards rise. Screens or curtains give some privacy from view but not from smells or noises.

Protecting people's privacy and security means residents being able to close and preferably lock their own doors. Sometimes there are fears about safety associated with locked doors, but there are designs of lock which can be opened from the outside in an emergency. When you are busy, it is important not to forget that closing bathroom and toilet doors is of basic importance in preserving a resident's dignity. Self-esteem, the value someone places on themselves, is easily damaged by the way they are treated. Residents whose dignity and privacy are not protected, can quite quickly accept it as a normal aspect of living in a care home. They may not complain because they have lost their former identity and self-worth through the poor care they have received.

Death and dying

When you are working in a care home death and dying are inevitable. Death, however, is never routine or commonplace for the person concerned and their family.

Raoul explains how death and dying are managed with dignity in the home where he works:

Raoul, team leader, residential home

When clients first join us they have to fill in a lengthy questionnaire to give us all the information we need including what they want us to do in the event of their death. It is much easier to ask these questions when someone is still reasonably fit. When we suspect that someone is dying we make sure that keyworkers always go into their room in pairs so that if they discover a body they are not on their own. At the point where someone is going downhill we make sure that all the staff are aware, by phoning them all at home if necessary and we explain to the other clients that the person is very ill.

Confidentiality is a problem in an environment where everyone is together but we do all we can to respect confidentiality for the client by not saying more than necessary. But it is important that death is not swept under the carpet. We put up notices in the event, so that people can go to funerals if they want to and we invite the family to have sandwiches and so on with us on the day if they want to do that. Rather than move someone when they are ill, if we think we can cope, we prefer to get agency nurses in and keep them with us for as long as possible. But we have a close relationship with a local nursing home and sometimes people transfer if it is the best thing for them.

If a keyworker has not been with someone before when they are dying then I spend time with them one to one explaining what is happening and why. We had someone recently who just gave up the will to live and her keyworker was distressed that we were not prepared to force her to eat. We had to explain that it was the client's choice. Our role is to support them in that choice and do what we can to continue to give them quality care. Every keyworker has different religious beliefs and that can affect how they feel about dying. In that particular case it was part of the keyworker's religious belief that no one had the right to choose to die. So she found this very difficult.

I will support keyworkers in saying goodbye to someone who has died so that they can see that a dead body isn't frightening. Because we have talked them through the process there doesn't seem to be a need for bereavement counselling afterwards, perhaps because it isn't a shock.

The important things which we might pick out of this account are:

- making sure that the home knows what residents want long before they become seriously ill
- keeping everyone as fully informed as possible while maintaining privacy
- not 'sweeping death under the carpet'

- allowing residents and staff to grieve for someone they have become attached to
- taking account of each person's religious beliefs and cultural preferences (see also Chapter 6)
- supporting and joining with the family during and after the death

Using preferred names

It has become common practice now for people to use first names from the point where they meet for the first time, but not everyone feels comfortable with this practice. Some people see informality as rudeness, particularly from someone who is younger than they are. Other people are not used to being addressed as Mr or Miss and feel formality is not necessary, particularly in what has become their own home. Thus it will be important for you to find out what name each resident prefers you to use. You can't just rely on the name that other care staff use. Residents should always be treated as adults and not like children. In some homes staff adopt a patronising attitude towards residents which is shown in the terms they use when they talk to them, such as 'love' or 'dear'. It is probably better to find out for yourself what people want you to call them by talking about it with each person.

Confidentiality and being discreet

Personal information is valuable. To be able to do your job properly you need to know quite a lot about the people you are caring for. When residents tell you something in confidence they should be able to expect that you won't pass it on to someone else. When you want to make conversation with someone it will be important not to talk about other residents or incidents which have happened to you at work involving other people.

Every care home keeps files about residents and staff. These have to be kept private and confidential so that only a limited number of people can see them. There are two laws which you need to be aware of: The Data Protection Act 1988 and The Access to Health Records Act 1990. Care homes must notify the Data Protection Commissioner about the records which they keep about people and allow those people to see the information kept. One person who has the right to see their file is the person themselves. This applies as much to you as a member of staff as it does to residents. You or a resident have a right to see any file kept on you and check that the information is accurate. The information on residents is not to be shared with relatives and friends without the resident's consent. Inspection Officers have a right to see personal files to check that they are being kept correctly and that the home is being run properly. The only other times when personal information can be shared is with health professionals in emergencies.

Think for a moment about the kind of situations where you think you might need to tell someone in authority personal information about a resident.

Perhaps you thought of some of the following:

- if you become aware that someone is doing something illegal or potentially dangerous like taking drugs or lighting fires
- if you think someone is contemplating suicide
- in cases where you suspect abuse (see Chapter 12)

So you may have to breach confidentiality in certain circumstances. It is not always clear-cut or easy to make decisions like this but it is something you could talk to your manager about.

Personal relationships

Most of us value our relationships with others and particularly with close friends and partners. Our need for intimacy may fluctuate throughout our lives but older people have a similar need for emotional, physical and sexual expression as any other member of the population.

Couples may find it difficult to have the privacy they need in a care home. Initiating, maintaining or ending relationships will inevitably be more difficult under the curious gaze of fellow residents. As a care assistant it is part of your role to do what you can to give residents the privacy they need in personal relationships. Couples can fall out and disagree when they are old just the same as young people. Marion's example is of two different couples:

Marion, senior care assistant, residential home

We've got one married couple just moved in – she used to work in the theatre. They each have their own room at opposite ends of the corridor because they argue. Just because you're married to some-one doesn't mean you don't want your own space sometimes.

When we had a married couple before, they had their own suite of rooms which was like two rooms next to each other and an en suite bathroom but they used one of the bedrooms as a sitting room. It was okay with the registration officer because they still had two rooms. If they both wanted to sleep in the same one that was up to them really. We put them on the top floor so they had a bit of privacy but after he died she wanted to come down and join in more. It was good she had all of us to turn to then so she wasn't so lonely. She'd spent years looking after him and now he's died, she's taken on a new lease of life.

The home where Marion works made a point of finding out what each couple wanted and didn't make any assumptions about what was right for them. As care assistant, it is obviously not your place to interfere in personal relationships whether couples are married or not. The area where care staff have a responsibility to intervene is where you suspect that a vulnerable resident is being exploited (see Chapter 12).

Personal belongings, hygiene and self-esteem

When we feel we look good it helps to maintain self-confidence. For most people, wearing the right clothes, having a hairdo and keeping clean are important aspects of our self-image: the way we see our-selves. Buying new fashionable and smart clothes, choosing what to wear, and being able to keep them well laundered, can be just as important to older people as it is to anyone else. On the other hand, other people may be comfortable in loose clothing or an old familiar sweater that is past its best.

Wearing other people's clothes, which may sometimes happen between relatives in a family, is not normally acceptable in a care home. This means that if clothes are laundered together they will need to be discreetly marked to make sure that they get back to the right person. It also means making sure that residents have the opportunity to shop for clothes of their choice and have sufficient storage space to keep them.

Think for a moment about what you would do if someone you were caring for decided not to have a bath for several weeks. This is quite a difficult one to solve because there are rights and responsibilities involved in this problem. Residents have a right to choose their own lifestyle. However, someone who chooses not to shave, wash or wear their dentures, will affect the way other people want to live. So, while individuals have a right to choose what they wear and how often they wash, they also have obligations towards other people in the group. There has to be a balance between rights and obligations if dignity is to be preserved.

This is also true in everyday life between neighbours. If someone in their own home lives in a way which creates a serious nuisance to other people, for example through excessive noise or through encouraging vermin, then action can be taken by the local authority. If a resident in a care home refuses to keep clean, it becomes an issue for others. It may also be a sign that the person themselves has lost their self-esteem.

KEY POINTS

- Group living brings with it the fear that other people will find out about our personal habits.
- If you are able to appear unembarrassed about touch and nakedness then the resident is less likely to be embarrassed too.
- Residents whose dignity and privacy are not protected can quite quickly accept it as a normal aspect of living in a care home. They may not complain because they have lost their former identity and self-worth through the poor care they have received.
- Death and dying are inevitable for all of us but death is never routine or commonplace for the person concerned and their family. Death should not be 'swept under the carpet'.
- You need to find out for yourself what name each person wants you to use when you talk to them. They may prefer first names or titles, like Mr or Mrs.
- Personal information is valuable. Residents should be able to expect that if they tell you something you will not pass it on to anyone else.
- Older people have a similar need for emotional, physical and sexual expression as any other member of the population.
- Looking good and keeping clean are important aspects of maintaining dignity and self-esteem for most people.

5 Encouraging Independence

It is sometimes quite difficult to take the time to help someone to do things for themselves especially if you are in a hurry. In this chapter we will look at:

- *Care planning and consistency of care*
- *Encouraging and helping residents to do things for themselves*
- *Promoting mobility*
- *Developing and preserving skills and abilities*
- *Socialising and maintaining links with the outside world*
- *Visitors and outings*

Care planning and consistency of care

A care plan is a written description of the social and health care which someone needs. It is based on an assessment of many aspects of the person's life. Nurses and care managers sometimes describe the assessment as 'holistic' because it should cover everything about that person.

Care plans will include personal details such as: previous address, date of birth, relatives, next of kin and important telephone numbers (such as own GP and social services care manager if there is one).

Care plans should:

- include information about the level of care that will be suitable
- describe how abilities and activities should be maintained
- propose targets for improvement where appropriate
- include details of the resident's preferences, such as particular food they like or dislike or what time they like to get up

- record the help needed with everyday activities and preferences on how that help should be given
- be regularly reviewed to take account of changing health and social care needs
- contain social contacts such as places and people of significance, previous work and family interests, particular friends or relatives who wish to continue to play a part in their life
- record risk assessments for different aspects such as safety, manual handling or pressure sores
- record medical history and any prescribed medicines
- outline nursing care, such as changing dressings for leg ulcers
- record any other treatments which have been arranged, such as physiotherapy
- include religious and cultural needs and any associated information such as significant events and dietary wishes
- describe how the person wishes the home to respond to death and dying

In a nursing home care plans would probably be drawn up by a registered nurse, following their nursing assessment. In some homes the nurses deal with all aspects of care planning but in others the care assistants may take on the role of monitoring care plans, recording progress and reviewing short-term and long-term goals. In a residential home it is less likely that nurses will be employed and so care assistants will probably keep the care plans. This is the view of one nursing home manager:

Francine, manager, nursing home

The care assistant is one of the most important people to the residents because they have the closest contact. We ask care assistants to do the most intimate things for residents and we should recognise that and value it. One fundamental way in which I disagree with many of my nursing colleagues is that I think properly trained and valued care assistants can be trusted to do the paperwork. Some of my colleagues think that care plans should only be updated

> by qualified nurses. If I can trust a care assistant to bath a resident then I think I can also trust her to write about that in the resident's record.

Francine talks about care plans being drawn up initially and updated as time goes by. Care needs may change over time so care plans need to be constantly reviewed and updated. This is Stella's experience of care which shows how much her care needs have changed since she moved in:

Stella, resident, residential home

I came here in November 1993 because I had hip trouble and couldn't get about. I had my hip replacement in March 1995 and since then I have been quite self-sufficient. I can walk without a stick. So the care staff don't have to do much for me really apart from make the bed and give me a fresh jug of water each day. I was a teacher for 43 years and lived on my own for 13 years after my husband died. So I am quite used to looking after myself. I don't need help with getting dressed but I don't think I could get in and out of the bath by myself anymore. I did a lot of sport when I was younger and I think I wore my joints out.

If you were looking after Stella you would need to:

- notice that she is able to do more for herself;
- keep a record of her progress; *and*
- help her to improve her skills and mobility.

Encouraging and helping residents to do things for themselves

As a care assistant you should encourage residents to be as independent as possible in caring for themselves. The balance of help and encouragement will be different for each resident and should be discussed with them. Ask if someone needs help and be sympathetic if a resident gets frustrated about not being able to help themselves. Fastenings such as buttons or awkwardly placed zips may become difficult for arthritic fingers and stiff joints. You could suggest trying out alternatives such as front openings or looser clothing without fastenings at all. If you have a number of residents to assist with washing and dressing in the mornings in a limited time, it will be helpful to you in the long term if you can maintain and maximise their ability to do things for themselves. When the residents remain independent for as long as possible, it helps to maintain their self-esteem and dignity.

If someone refuses to dress or undress and if coaxing and gentle persuasion do not alter the situation then you should respect the resident's choice. However, if this is unusual then you should be aware that there may be something wrong, such as illness. Sometimes just leaving the situation and returning later to try again may be all that is needed.

Promoting mobility

As we get older, our muscles tend to lose their strength and bones lose calcium and tend to become more fragile. General wear and tear on the body can affect residents' ability and willingness to move about. Encouraging mobility will mean using different approaches for different people. It will also involve being flexible with each individual according to how they are feeling that day. Someone who is tired, perhaps at the end of a day, may need greater support in moving about than they do first thing in the morning. People's needs also change over time.

Individual targets for increasing or maintaining mobility should be in each care plan. Some care homes take a pride in promoting mobility:

Pam, owner, nursing home

We have a culture of rehabilitation here which means that our aim is to maximise potential. We were able to send a resident home recently. She came to us after surgery with very little mobility but within a few weeks we had her walking again and able to manage on her own. So she went home, which was great.

It is a mistake to give too much help. For example:

- it is better to show someone how to get out of a well-designed chair by themselves than immediately offer a helping hand
- walk alongside someone without supporting them but with your arm available if they are unsure
- do not use wheelchairs merely to save time
- know when to offer moral support and encouragement rather than physical support
- make sure that, if someone uses a walking frame, it is kept within their reach.

One of the areas of health and safety in which your employer should provide training is how to protect yourself, and particularly your back, when you are mobilising residents. Normally it should be possible to avoid actually lifting someone, particularly if the home has the proper equipment such as hoists. Where lifting weights is unavoidable then this should normally involve two care staff working together and using their bodies in a way which doesn't damage them.

Developing and preserving skills and abilities

Some care homes have developed innovative ideas for stimulating residents. The next case example is a nursing home where the idea of putting older people and young children together has been successfully tried:

Pat, manager, nursing home

We have a children's day nursery here. Six years ago we found we had some space on the top floor which was accessible by staircase but not suitable for nursing care so we looked into the possibility of opening a day nursery. The registration authority took some persuading but eventually they said we could give it a go and we haven't looked back since.

At first the two groups were quite separate but 1st October 1996 was International Day of the Older Person and we used that as a reason for introducing structured activities involving both groups. It was a success so we continued doing it. The residents have all the time in the world to spare and a lot of patience. I think older people are underutilised in society. They have so much to give and everyone needs a role in life. Some of the care staff have been able to use the nursery as a facility for their own children though we don't have babies, just two to five years. We also have families where the child has a great grandmother in the home and can come and visit her during the day. There is a South African child whose real grandparents are abroad and who enjoys the 'surrogate grandparenting' provided by our residents. When his mum comes to pick him up he says: "I've been playing with my grannies today." We have some people without legs or who can't communicate and the children seem to simply accept them, even to have empathy. They may ask questions about why Tom can't speak so I explain that he has had a stroke and they accept that.

I worried that the risk of mixing the two groups would be germs but so far this has not been a problem at all. Bringing the two groups together is a good chance to have fun. People live till they die here. Sometimes they find themselves doing all sorts of things that they have never done before.

We have regular visitors from the 'Pat a dog' scheme and one gentleman said he didn't like dogs because he had lived abroad and always associated them with rabies. He said he'd rather stroke a camel. So we contacted a circus and they brought a whole collection of smallish animals along with a clown and both groups, adults and children, enjoyed the event. It was good publicity for them of course.

Then we had a Scottish dancing display for the residents and the children came to watch too. The children made red nose cakes for Red Nose Day and sold them to the residents to raise funds for the nursery. When I bought a new dog my friend who is a dog trainer came along and did a training class with him so that both groups could watch. The adults liked watching the children's faces.

We have one gentleman who misses his grandchildren and when it was his birthday eight children came down to present him with his birthday cake and sing happy birthday to him which he loved. Happy people are easier to deal with. They want to join in: it is something to talk about other than their aches and pains or their bowels. The death rate is very low here. I think that is a good sign that people are happy. Sometimes I think people just turn their faces to the wall and die unless you can give them something to live for.

As you can see, this care home has put a lot of thought into providing the kind of stimulating activities which will help to develop and maintain residents' skills and abilities. Appendix 2 on page 133 shows just one sample week of the kind of activities that they provide for residents every week of the year. The Age Concern publication *The Successful Activity Co-ordinator's Training Pack* (see p 147) gives further ideas.

Socialising and maintaining links with the outside world

We are social beings and most people have a large network of other people, relatives or friends, who play a part in their lives. Think for a moment of some of the people who are important in your life.

Perhaps you thought of relatives such as parents, brothers and sisters, children and partners. There may be lots of other people too who are friends or neighbours. You may have known them only a short time or for a long time. Perhaps you have been able to keep in contact throughout your life so far with friends you made when you were a child.

Telephones can be a good way for residents to keep in touch. Many care homes arrange for residents to have their own telephone point in their bedroom. Josie talks here about the way that telephones are used to promote socialising in the home where she works:

Josie, head of care, residential home

Each room has a telephone which they can use to talk to the kitchen if they want a snack or a cup of tea. They can talk to each other with them: "I'm going out in the garden – do you want to come?" And they can phone out, so it is a total communication system. The call bells are only for emergencies. Because they aren't used very often we always respond quickly because we know it must be important.

As a care assistant you will probably meet relatives and friends of residents whenever they visit. It will be helpful for you to establish friendly relationships with all the significant people in the lives of the people you care for. It will help you to get to know them and their care needs better.

Some homes encourage relatives to join a support group linked with the home in a formal way. A relatives' group would probably meet regularly to discuss life in the home and ways in which they can contribute to it. Perhaps relatives can help out by providing transport for outings or by fund-raising or running special events for residents. There is a Relatives and Residents Association (for details see p 140) which supports relatives and relatives' groups.

If you talk to older people about their networks you may find that they have no living relatives or have lost contact with them. Some older people live very isolated lives. This may be because they are afraid to go out or find it difficult to join clubs and seek out new friendships when the people close to them have died. Although many people are reluctant to give up their own homes, for some a care home can offer a greater quality of life in terms of social relationships. Here there is a place to form close and real friendships with people who enjoy doing the same things or have similar experiences of life.

People in a group sometimes behave differently from the way they behave as individuals outside the group. Someone who was previously silent and solitary may become socially significant and valued by the group. This may be because of their personality or the qualities they bring to the lives of others.

Life in a care home can become very separate from life outside unless contact with the outside world is consciously promoted. Here are two examples of ways homes can achieve this:

Joan, team leader, residential home

We've got a hydrotherapy pool here in the studio which is separate from the main house, and we run all sorts of classes which the public can come to as well. So it's important for keyworkers to let their clients know what's happening. We take the minibus into the city on Tuesdays so people can go shopping in the big shops and most people want to go, though of course they don't have to if they don't want to. We make sure they are accompanied if they need it. There is an in-house trolley shop for those who prefer not to go and we have a clothes show from time to time. It's one of the local stores who come so the clothes are good quality and people can try them on and choose what they want. Some families buy clothes for clients too. We have a reflexologist and aromatherapist calling but very few people use them, perhaps because it is a new idea they are not used to.

Pam, owner, nursing home

Contact with the outside world has taken on a new dimension for our residents with the introduction of computers. We've got a computer project worker here at the moment. She's an American nurse on a graduate placement scheme doing work with the residents and the staff. What we wanted was to provide internet access so that people with relatives abroad can communicate with them by e-mail. We also have a virtual reality gardening package which is creating a lot of interest. I'm keen to see the care staff looking at distance learning this way too as an alternative to going to college.

These two care homes bring people in and encourage residents to look outwards but in very different ways. One provides encouragement for the local community to share the facilities and the other provides contact through information technology.

Visitors and outings

Relatives, friends and other visitors should always be welcome in a care home. Some homes prefer visitors to come at times when they are less busy, such as in the afternoons. But others are much more relaxed and feel people should be able to come and go as they please.

Joan, team leader, residential home

We don't have a guest room unfortunately but visitors can come in for a meal anytime they want and if someone's dying we'd always manage to find somewhere for their relatives to sleep. I always say visiting is 24 hours a day here. Not everyone can get away during the day and why shouldn't they come when it suits them?

Visitors provide important contact with the outside world and can stimulate activity. Short walks or wheelchair rides can make a change from sitting outside in the garden in fine weather. Some care homes will organise activities within the home but there should also be opportunities to go to social clubs, pubs or shops on a regular basis. Your role in organising or being involved in these activities will vary from one home to another.

Outings to places of interest provide a change of scene. Here are some case examples from care homes to show the variety possible:

Paula, care assistant, residential home

We tried strawberry picking once – that was a laugh. I don't know how many of the strawberries were edible by the end of it. We sometimes get people who are interested in gardening. One man had a propagator in the conservatory so he could grow things. Another lady had a herb garden in an old sink. We sometimes take people to the theatre or down to the pub. We've got a minibus so we can take people into town shopping. Or we can take people out to lunch sometimes. So there's a lot going on.

June, team leader, residential home

The residents all do different things here. There's no call for group activities really. One or two go to church. A vicar comes once a fortnight for Communion for the four who want it. Most people prefer to spend the day on their own in their rooms. They don't all sit round the edge of the day room here staring at the television. Lots of people prefer their own company. They may have lived on their own for years and just aren't sociable.

Some have visitors. Lots of the residents come from the local area and have friends who live locally who come and visit them. Irene comes from the village and used to be in the warden assisted flats. She has friends come to visit nearly every day from there. Some go up to the village hairdresser and to the post office. They go to some things in the village like the club at the village hall where they play table games. Some go for walks round the village; one lady has a bus pass and goes into the city a lot now her husband has died. She looked after him for years and couldn't get out much. Now she's making the most of life, exploring the city with her new found freedom.

Some people knit squares for blankets. They made one for the refugees. We had a sale of work downstairs in the hallway last year and made some money for outings.

Lily is going to her sister's for three weeks holiday this year. Most people go out for days with their family now and again.

Four people went to the Music Hall at the Winter Gardens last Saturday. We took them in our cars. We've got a beach hut on the coast too, which is accessible for wheelchairs, but the toilets are about 50 yards away across the pebbles, which is a bit of a problem when you are in a hurry!

Some people like helping round the house: changing jugs of water or helping in the kitchen. They can use the kitchen when the cook isn't there but it is at their own risk. One likes washing up and peeling vegetables. But lots of people don't want to do anything really. They say they have worked all their life and they just want a rest.

KEY POINTS

- A care plan is a written description of the social and health care which someone needs. It should be based on a holistic assessment of many aspects of the person's life and kept up to date.
- As a care assistant you should encourage residents to be as independent as possible in caring for themselves.
- Individual targets for increasing or maintaining mobility should be in each care plan.
- Stimulating activities can encourage new skills and abilities as well as preserve existing ones.
- For some people life in a care home can provide a greater quality of life in terms of social relationships.
- It is important to encourage residents to look outwards and develop and maintain their contacts with the outside world.
- Visitors and outings provide important contact and can stimulate activity.

6 Valuing Individuality and Difference

In a group setting like a care home it is important for each resident to be able to maintain their own personal identity. The ideas we will look at in this chapter include:

- *Equal opportunities*
- *Racial identity*
- *Ethnic origin*
- *Religion*
- *Cultural identity*
- *Valuing difference*

Equal opportunities

Each of us has our own lifestyle. This is a word which describes all aspects of the way we live. This might show in:

- the time you get up or go to bed
- what you do in your spare time and who your friends are
- whether you have your main meal at midday or in the evening and what kind of food you like to eat
- the kind of clothes you wear and how you wear your hair
- whether you practise any religion
- whether you belong to a close-knit family that sees a lot of each other or perhaps only meet up for weddings and funerals
- whether you go out a lot or spend more time at home watching TV or reading a book

Our lifestyles are to some extent influenced by advertising and the way other people around us live, but the strongest influence on lifestyle is probably the way we were brought up.

Many care homes have an equal opportunities policy which sets out the home's intentions to treat everyone fairly. The policy might for example state: what the care home believes in the area of equality; and how the residents and staff are entitled to be treated.

Equal opportunities ought to be included in all of the care home's practice so that particular individuals are not disadvantaged or excluded because of their:

- age
- disability
- race or colour
- culture
- ethnic origin
- religion
- class
- gender
- marital status
- sexual orientation

There is legislation which covers the way staff are recruited and selected for jobs to make sure that everyone gets an equal chance to work. Equal opportunities policies in a care home should also cover aspects of the way residents are treated and the way that people relate to one another in the workplace.

Racial identity

When we talk about someone's racial identity we usually mean their colour. Black is a term which is used to describe the colour of someone's skin; it is also a political term for people who experience racism.

Racism is a word to describe racial prejudice (meaning negative attitudes and beliefs about people based on their skin colour), as well as racial discrimination (meaning unfair behaviour towards a group of people because of their skin colour). Racism is about the abuse of power in society. In the UK white people have more power than black people. Because of racism, black people experience discrimination and disadvantage in their everyday lives. This shows in education, housing, the legal system and the way health and social care services are provided as well as in access to work.

Some people prefer to live in residential homes run by people who share the same racial identity as themselves but this is not true for everyone. In many areas of the UK, there is insufficient choice of care homes for this to be possible. There are also care homes run by black owners and managers where many of the residents are white.

As a care assistant it will be important for you to try to increase your understanding of the causes and effects of racism and the significance of racial identity.

Ethnic origin

Ethnic origin is a term used to describe the group you belong to. If you are white you might see yourself as Irish, Welsh or Scottish for example. Sometimes ethnicity is so closely allied to religion that the two cannot be easily separated. For example the word Jewish is used for both ethnic origin and religion. Here's an example from Sean of how he feels about his ethnic identity:

> **Sean, resident in sheltered accommodation with extra care**
>
> I came to London from Dublin in 1944 thinking I was going to get rich and then go back home but it didn't turn out quite like that. I'll never return now. I don't know anyone there now. I'd have to make all new friends again. What I like about this place is they're all Irish here: the residents and the staff. Of course we do all those things together, like celebrate St Patrick's Day, but it's more than that. It goes much deeper. When you meet your own it is easier to talk to them than to a stranger. We speak the same language even though it's English, if you know what I mean. Just because we look the same doesn't mean we feel the same.

Sean's ethnic origin is important to him and the people who care for him need to understand that and take it into account.

Religion

Religion is about spiritual beliefs and faith. Hinduism, Sikhism, Judaism and Christianity are examples of religious faiths. Spiritual needs are just as important as any other needs. Many care homes arrange for religious leaders to visit residents and perhaps hold services on the premises. It is easy to forget that other people may have different religious beliefs from our own or may not want to take part at all. Religion will probably also determine the way we want to be dealt with when we die.

Cultural identity

Culture is the collection of customs and beliefs of a group of people expressed through such things as the art, writing, music and architecture which they produce. If we look at the paintings and drawings of the Aboriginal people of Australia, for example, we can understand something of their history and religious beliefs because their paintings reflect their culture.

Valuing difference

All of these factors – race, ethnic origin, religious faith, and culture – can affect:

- the way people bring up their children
- attitudes towards relationships, for example marriage
- the food eaten and the way it is cooked
- the clothes worn, for example if particular parts of the body need to be kept covered
- the frequency of washing or the choices made between showers or baths
- the events celebrated, each day, week or year

They should also influence the way someone is cared for if they become a resident in a care home.

Living in a group inevitably involves making some compromises. But one of your important roles as care assistant will be to find out

residents' preferences and do everything you can to help them maintain their former way of life. This is not always easy, as June
describes in this case example:

June, team leader, residential home

What we say is we try to change someone's address but not their
lifestyle. The trouble is that most of the people who come here
have already lost a lot of their former lifestyle. They've probably
given up many of their social activities. Because of what's happening to their minds they don't know who anyone is any more.

Lots of the residents don't go to church but then a lot of them
probably never did. Most of our clients with dementia, even those
who used to go to church, have lost that by the time they come
here. We have a non-denominational chaplain who comes in once
a week to talk to anyone who wants him. Then the Catholic priest
comes to give Communion too. One daughter comes and takes her
mother to church every week but I don't know how much she gets
out of it now. Then there's the man who played in a mission band.
They arranged to have him picked up and taken to listen to the
band perform after he couldn't play any more. That was nice and
he enjoyed that.

We have a Mormon lady at the moment and her family helped us
with her dietary needs because there are certain things she wasn't
supposed to have like tea and coffee. But we have lots of discus-
sions about this one. She herself is suffering from dementia and
asks for a cup of tea when everyone else has one. She really wants
one because I suppose she has forgotten that it's not allowed and
it's very hard for us to decide what to do. If you can't have something you're not supposed to have when you're 93, when can you?
I sometimes ask myself: what are we saving this person for? But
her family would be upset if they thought she was not sticking to
their religious principles.

Getting to know how to deal with those kind of situations is something you have to learn from experience.

The important points highlighted by June's account, involving people with dementia, are:

- It is difficult to know what is going through someone's mind when they are suffering from dementia, for example whether they are still understanding or enjoying a religious experience.
- It is difficult to decide what is best for someone who has lost the ability to make decisions.
- The wishes of relatives and the requirements of religious observance must be taken into account when the resident has forgotten.

These are the kind of issues which you need to be aware of as a care assistant. Most of the people you care for will probably not be suffering from dementia and a sense of continuity will be important in their lives. It is closely linked with our identity – how we see ourselves. So you can find out their preferences by asking questions, to make sure, as far as possible, that the residents can live the kind of life they want to live. You may also want to share something of your own life with residents so that they see you as an individual too.

The principle of valuing difference is that each person should be treated as unique. The principles of care apply to people of all cultures, religions, sexuality, race or ethnic group. Equality does not mean sameness. It is not appropriate to treat people with different needs in the same way. This means paying as much attention to residents' cultural, racial, ethnic or religious needs as you do to their physical health. To make sure that older people get the service they are entitled to you should pay particular attention to the following:

Language – when someone speaks more than one language, they might find it difficult to express exactly what they want to say in English. In some areas relatives may be able to help or there may be a local interpreting service. Never assume that you understand what is being said unless you are sure. If you have tried to learn another language, perhaps when you were at school, you may understand how difficult it is to become fluent. If you can learn a few words of a resident's other language it may help them to feel more at home.

Culture and religion – find out as much as you can about important religious days and events in other cultures and help residents to observe them if they want to. Christmas can be a difficult time for people who do not wish to celebrate it. However, many people of other faiths do enjoy Christmas as a secular event when people give each other presents and have parties. Never make assumptions about festivals and events which to you may seem an ordinary part of your life.

Activities – residents may want to take part in activities organised outside the home, by others who share the same culture, language, religion or ethnic origin. Never assume that this is the case, but if you know of activities taking place which you think a resident might be interested in, make sure they have information about it and ask whether they want to join in. Perhaps they would like you to make contact with a local community activity and arrange informal contact for them.

Meals – find out about the choices which people want to make not only about their diet but also about the way they want to eat; for example cutlery can be used in different ways or not used, some residents may prefer to eat alone, or there may be conventions about hygiene which you were not previously aware of.

Clothing – if you are helping someone to dress or undress you may need to learn how to manage and care for a sari, for example, and know what is appropriate for different occasions, such as whether someone normally keeps their head covered in public.

Challenge stereotyping – it is a good idea to learn as much as you can about other cultures but do not make assumptions about people. The best approach is to treat each resident and their family as the experts on their own culture.

Washing – we each become accustomed to a routine of keeping clean through washing. However, this routine varies from one family to another and from one culture to another. In some hot countries it is common to wash or shower and change one's clothes several times a day and people can feel very uncomfortable or dirty if they can't follow their normal routine. Many religions require washing at particular times such as before prayer or before getting out of bed or after using the lavatory.

Intimate care, touch and gender – rules about modesty in the way we dress or behave is something we may take for granted but normal codes of behaviour vary enormously. It can be very difficult for someone who observes strict codes of modesty to allow themselves to be touched, especially by a member of the opposite sex. Be sensitive to the issues and find out what is acceptable to the person you are caring for.

Death and dying – attitudes towards death and dying are very individual and strongly influenced by culture and religion. For example, the teaching of all the major religions is that death is not the end but there is wide variation in beliefs about what happens after death. Someone who is dying may have a whole range of care needs including emotional and spiritual needs as well as physical ones. Think also about your own reactions and responses to the situation because that will affect your ability to provide care.

The Age Concern book *Culture, Religion and Patient Care in a Multi-Ethnic Society: A handbook for professionals* has more information about meeting different religious and cultural needs (see pp 146–147).

KEY POINTS

- Each of us has our own lifestyle which is influenced by the way we were brought up.
- An equal opportunities policy sets out the home's intentions to treat everyone fairly.
- Prejudice is negative attitudes and beliefs about people based on, for example, their skin colour, sexuality, ethnic origin, religion or culture.
- Racial discrimination is unfair behaviour towards a group of people based on prejudice.
- It is an important aspect of a care assistant's role to help residents maintain their former way of life as far as possible.
- Equality does not mean sameness. It is not appropriate to treat people with different needs in the same way.
- The principle of valuing difference is that each person should be treated as unique.

7 | Promoting Choice and Self-esteem

In this chapter we will look at ways of making sure we find out what choices residents want to make and how you can help them to feel in control of their own lives. The areas we particularly focus on include:

- *Promoting self-esteem*
- *Involvement in decision making*
- *Expressing preferences and advocacy*
- *Timetables and routines*
- *Meals and mealtimes*
- *Pets as therapy*

Promoting self-esteem

When we think about care needs, most of us would remember the basic physical things which people need to survive: food; drink; sleep; and warmth. But there is a lot more to care than these. A psychologist called Abraham Maslow drew up a diagram (see p 72) to express the different needs which we have and he put them in a pyramid in order of importance. He said that basic needs have to be met before anything else but beyond those there are other needs which are just as important.

Self-esteem is the value which someone places on themselves. It depends to a great extent on the way we are treated by others. As a care assistant you have an important role in promoting residents' self-esteem by helping them to feel good about themselves.

Maslow's Hierarchy of Needs

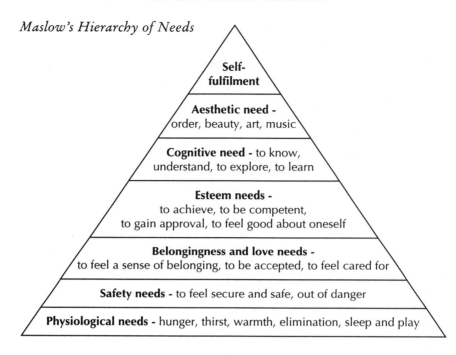

Pat, manager, nursing home

We get lots of visitors here so it is important that the care staff always look their best. It encourages them to put on their bit of make-up and keep clean and tidy, and that makes the residents feel valued too. So they dress up and look their best too. We are always in the paper or on television doing something new and different. I think the fact that this home has a good reputation and is well-known locally boosts the residents' self-esteem.

Involvement in decision making

Part of your role as care assistant is to keep residents informed about what is happening both in the home and in the wider community so that they can take part. Some homes will also have noticeboards and newsletters to promote communication but personal contact usually works best.

Dan, team leader, residential home

What we do well here is promote client choice. We wouldn't dream of moving someone out of their room without asking them, for example. We haven't got any rules really except for the smoking one. But that's for health and safety. We don't let them smoke in their bedrooms but there are lots of other places in the building where they can have a cigarette if they want. You can't expect someone who has smoked all their life to give it up but, on the other hand, we don't want the building burnt down.

And there's lots of food things. We have a menu because you have to, but we often go down the harbour and buy a few cockles or a herring for someone who wants it special. If they want a cup of tea and toast at 2am they can have it. If people want to lie on their beds in the daytime then of course they can. I know lots of places where they can't do what they want.

We've got a committee which meets to talk about how to spend the amenity fund. There's a retired assistant manager who chairs it, there's some day centre clients, the vicar and a few staff as well as some of the residents. They talk about things the clients want like a new TV or fans for the hot weather. They also notice if we haven't had something on the menu lately that they like.

Dan stressed how important he thought it was that residents and their families and friends have a say in how the home is run. The home where Dan works has a formal committee to discuss events and make decisions about future plans. As not everyone likes committees, informal conversations over meals, on social occasions or at coffee time, can be just as effective in finding out people's views. More formal committees may include residents, relatives, staff and other members of the local community. In that case it would be important to make sure that the people who attend the meetings fully represent all the residents' views. Some large homes have 'Friends' organisations for relatives to fund-raise for outings. More formal meetings can be difficult to manage particularly where residents are very frail and find it difficult to join in. Whatever method the home uses, it is important that the residents feel that they have a real chance to influence the decisions being made about their lives.

Expressing preferences and advocacy

Some people feel that they have very little choice over their lives. They may have a disability which limits their movement or their ability to communicate with other people. Others may have very low incomes or other personal circumstances which limit what they can do. However, most of us can decide for ourselves where we go and what we do. Research studies show that feeling in control of life will have a strong effect on whether someone sees the service they receive as good quality.

Residents may want to influence lots of different aspects of life in the home, such as:

- the timetable and routines
- activities provided each day
- choice of meals and mealtimes
- whether they can come and go freely
- being able to move about the home as they want to
- being able to open a window for fresh air
- deciding what to wear

In a group setting there may be limitations on choice but it is part of your role as care assistant to do all you can to make sure residents have as much control as possible over their daily lives.

Sometimes people may need someone to act as advocate for them. An advocate is someone who speaks for or on behalf of someone else. It is a skilled role which is used where a resident has become unable to speak or communicate for themselves. In some areas of the country independent advocates are recruited and trained by local authorities or voluntary organisations, including Age Concern. Advocates are then available to come into a home and help promote good communication.

Timetables and routines

In most homes there are certain tasks which the manager aims to achieve each day and often these may be expressed as a timetable for care assistants, for example:

7am	start getting residents up and dressed
8am	start serving breakfast
9am	provide medication
10.30am	coffee etc

The most common example of routines in care homes is the times people get up in the morning, have a bath or go to bed at night. In other homes, however, the atmosphere is more relaxed and there is little feeling of being tied to a routine which cannot be varied.

If you are a new care assistant in a home where routines seem to rule and make it difficult for residents to choose their preferred way of life, you may find it hard to change what is happening. You may want to talk to your manager about introducing greater flexibility for residents. On the other hand, the way you approach your daily tasks and interact with residents will make a real difference to how they feel about their day.

Meals and mealtimes

Living in a group inevitably involves compromise. Let's look at family life as a form of group living. Think for a moment about the times in a family when you have to accept compromise around meals and mealtimes. Perhaps you thought of all or some of the following:

- You may have to eat food that has been chosen and cooked by someone else.
- The variety may be limited by shortage of money.
- Having a physical disability may limit what you are able to cook.
- Your body may react badly to particular kinds of food: perhaps, for example, you have an allergy to nuts.
- There may have to be set times of the day for meals, particularly if someone in the family is diabetic.

- You may have to wait for other members of the family to arrive home before you can eat together.

So your ability to choose has boundaries around it. In a care home it may be easier for staff if residents all eat in the same place and at the same time. It may be thought more economical if the choice of food is limited. But someone who wants to eat in their room should be allowed to do so. Another person may have gone out for part of a day and need a meal provided unusually early before they go or unusually late after they return. Flexibility to accommodate residents' individual choice of meals and mealtimes is vital to making them feel at home. Raoul explains how meals are dealt with in the care home where he works:

Raoul, team leader, residential home

Clients have a big say in the menus here. We have regular clients' meetings and a suggestion box which is well used. The hot food is laid out on a hot plate and cold food on a cool tray when people come into the dining room, so they can see it and choose what they want, like if they were in a restaurant. The care staff change their clothes and wait on table at mealtimes so they know if someone is not eating or needs help. After every meal the chef comes out of the kitchen and asks people about their meal and they put in requests.

The care home which Raoul describes is run rather like a hotel and the care staff wear uniforms like waitresses at mealtimes to help create an atmosphere of formality. The tables are well laid out with candles in the evenings and wine is available for those who want it. This kind of restaurant atmosphere is unusual in a care home but it is attractive to the residents here and most people choose to join in.

There are bound to be limitations on the choice of food which can be offered because of staff time and the costs involved but, wherever possible, residents should be able to eat food that they like. A balance also has to be drawn between the benefits of healthy eating and the pleasures of eating some of the foods which may not be good for you at all.

In some homes communal mealtimes have become a time for handing out medication or personal letters. This practice raises issues of privacy and dignity because everyone will know who is taking medicine and for what, or who has had another letter from a friend and who never gets letters at all. Meals and mealtimes need careful handling.

Pets as therapy

If you have pets yourself you will know how central they can become to our lives. For someone living alone, a dog, cat or caged bird can be an important member of the family. Dog walking also encourages owners to take regular exercise too.

Some homes will welcome residents' own pets while others may have pets which belong to the home. An indoor fish tank or a fish pond outside can be absorbing to watch because of the continuous movement. They have sometimes been used in places like hospitals and dentists' waiting rooms to calm patients at times of stress. In some areas local dog owners will bring their animals into a care home under national and local schemes for providing comfort to residents. Stroking an animal is very soothing and can satisfy some of our emotional needs.

There are lots of other kinds of animals which people keep, of course, and each home will have to decide which animals are welcome and which aren't.

> **Ken, residential home owner**
>
> That shed at the bottom of the garden is our pigeon loft. It was Bill who started it. He talked about when he was younger and always had racing pigeons about the place and I thought why not? So we got a second-hand shed and a few birds and it kept him happy for hours.

Eileen, inspection officer

They always have lots of pets at this particular care home I'm thinking of, and I think it's really nice for the residents. They are always good at making sure they keep the cats off the working surfaces and things like that so there are usually no hygiene problems. But I remember one occasion. It was lunchtime soon after I arrived that day, and when I looked into the dining room I noticed that everyone seemed to be crowded down one end of the room. There were two empty tables but the residents were all squashed round the others. Then I noticed the glass tank on the shelf up against the wall by the empty tables. It had this huge hairy spider in it and apparently they were all petrified of the thing and wouldn't go anywhere near it! Pets are all very well I said, but there are limits!

As a care assistant you may find yourself having to make it possible for pets to play a role in the life of the people you care for. It will probably mean ensuring that proper hygiene is maintained, for example keeping cats out of the kitchen and keeping outside spaces clean. It may also involve trying to minimise nuisance to other residents and being aware of whether the animal is properly fed and watered and getting its vaccinations. But a pet can make all the difference to a resident's life.

KEY POINTS

■ Self-esteem is the value which someone places on themselves.

■ It is important for residents to feel that they have a say in how the home is run. Some homes may have a residents' committee but there are other ways of finding out people's views and taking them into account.

■ In a group setting there may be limitations on choice but it is important that you do all you can to make sure that residents have as much control as possible over their lives.

■ Routines should be as flexible as possible and the way you approach your tasks will make all the difference to the way residents feel about their day.

■ Wherever possible residents should be able to eat the food they like, where and when they want it.

■ Pets can make a real difference to residents' lives.

8 Recognising Rights and Responsibilities

Residents in care homes have the same rights and similar responsibilities as any other member of society. The particular areas we will look at here are:

- *Residents' contracts with a home*
- *Complaints procedures*
- *Taking part in civil society*
- *Rights checklist*
- *Managing money*
- *Access to files*

Residents' contracts with a home

Some people pay their own fees when they move into a care home but it is more usual for places to be funded by a local authority – this happens after the person has been assessed as requiring residential care.

When a social services care manager makes an assessment of care needs they should provide a prospective resident with information about their rights. The information might include:

- how the social services department can help
- the arrangements for discharge from hospital, if that is appropriate
- a copy of the joint assessment and agreed care plan
- what to do if unhappy with the assessment or the help provided afterwards
- information about homes in the area and how to see their inspection reports

Providing residential care is often a triangular relationship involving:

- the resident;
- the care home; *and*
- the funder, ie a local authority social services department.

If the social services department is funding a residential place it would normally have a contract with the home to provide care. In some local authorities it is considered normal practice for the home also to have an agreement with the resident setting out the terms between them.

When someone agrees to move into a care home they lose the security that most people take for granted. If the move is expected to be permanent it is good practice for the home to try to provide a feeling of security through the resident's agreement. Residents need to know their rights of occupation and the responsibilities they have towards the other residents, owners and staff of the home. This might be written down as a formal contract which both parties sign. The agreement would also set out what residents should do if they want to move somewhere else or if they become more frail and have to move to a different home which would meet their changed needs better.

As a care assistant you need to know what the contract says about the residents' rights and responsibilities. Contracts are normally kept on each resident's file and you might expect to have their significance explained to you as part of your induction.

Complaints procedures

If you have ever tried making a complaint about something you will know how difficult it is. Perhaps you have bought something and then found when you got it home that it was damaged or you may have been served a meal in a restaurant which was badly cooked. Think for a moment about a time when something like this happened to you. How did you feel about complaining?

Perhaps you felt intimidated by the situation and couldn't say anything even though you wanted to. If you managed to speak out, perhaps you felt very anxious about causing trouble. Many people find it so hard to complain about the service in a shop or restaurant that they are too embarrassed to use the service again. Imagine how much more difficult it must be if you are complaining about the service in the place which has become your home. If you are dependent on someone else for your care, that puts you in a very vulnerable position where you may feel afraid to speak out.

It is important that each home has a complaints procedure that makes it easy for residents and their relatives to make a complaint if they wish, without feeling bad about doing so. You can help to make it easier by your attitude about complaints. No one likes being complained about, but by welcoming complaints you can get good information about how to provide a better service.

> **Pek, head of care, residential home**
>
> We are here to minister to their every want. If there's something they want they can have it. We have residents' meetings every so often and we talk about how things are going and if there is anything they want to change. But they can always talk to me in private if they prefer. They have lots of access to the owners too and they're both good listeners. Of course we have a formal complaints procedure but usually we can sort things out without having to resort to formality.

Pek describes a situation where the care home welcomes residents' suggestions and accepts that they may want to change things. As care assistant it is part of your job to help residents express their views on every aspect of life in the home and to see those views as positive and useful because they can help shape the service you provide.

Taking part in civil society

Every citizen has rights and responsibilities in society. These include voting in elections. Someone who is living in a care home may have difficulty getting the sort of information which political parties provide at election times. They may also need help in getting to a polling station or in voting by post or proxy. Let's look at the way June does that:

June, team leader, residential home

We didn't get many people who voted at the last election: just two went to the polling station and two had postal votes. But we give them the papers and explain what's happening but most people don't bother. The important thing is that we let them know that they could if they wanted to. I noticed none of the candidates came knocking on our door. Perhaps if they knew we had 35 potential supporters for them they might have come in and tried to convert them.

As June says, the important things are:

- making sure people have the information they need;
- helping them to carry out a postal vote (or proxy vote) if that is the method they want to use; *and*
- arranging transport for those who want to go to the polling station.

When it comes to citizens' rights and responsibilities, voting in elections isn't the whole story of course. Residents can contribute to society in many ways just as any other member of the public. Alice Settle is an example of someone who has continued to contribute significantly to the life of her village from her room in a residential home:

Marion, senior care assistant, residential home

Did you notice the new bit of pavement between here and the pub and the post office? One of our residents, Alice Settle, did that. She pestered the Council until they did up the pavement because it was so dangerous: you had to walk on the road. It's been like it for years and gradually got worse and worse. She wrote to them and complained, insisted on her rights and single-handedly badgered them into doing something about it.

In other care homes residents continue to express their concern for people who are less fortunate then themselves by fund-raising for charity or making blankets for example. By doing these sorts of things for other people they are able to feel that they are still useful members of society and still have a contribution to make.

Rights checklist

Residents in a care home have rights. The following list, which is based on the Kent County Council *Good Care* guide (see p 137), sets out some of the rights which residents should have in the care home where you work:

- Choosing how they want to be addressed.
- Having access to a range of specialist services.
- Choosing what they want to eat and drink as well as when and where they eat it.
- Having access to an advocate if they are unable to express themselves.
- Being treated as an individual.
- Belonging in their own home, for example privacy in their own room.
- Discussing and agreeing any changes in living arrangements.
- Being able to suggest improvements.
- Having visitors of their own choice.
- Having a clear residency agreement.
- Registering and voting in elections.
- Mixing with the local community.
- Choosing their own GP and dentist.
- Being independent without any unnecessary restrictions on their freedom of movement.
- Having respect for their cultural and religious needs.
- Caring for themselves whenever possible.

Perhaps you can think of others.

Managing money

Keeping control of your own money is an important part of being in control of your own life. Sometimes a care home will have arrangements for less mobile residents so that their pension is collected for them. Keeping good written records is vital to protect both the resident and you when money is changing hands. Privacy and security are very important too and you should try as far as you can to make sure that transactions take place in private. Having a lockable place to keep valuables like documents or jewellery, as well as money, will help residents to feel safe and secure.

Residents, just like any other member of the community, may have investments and property that they want to manage; sometimes banks, solicitors and other relevant professionals can make arrangements to visit individuals in the care home if that is what they want. People who are unable to manage their own finances may arrange for someone else to do that on their behalf.

Some homes have an amenity fund to spend for the benefit of all residents. Other homes may charge individuals for providing extra services such as outings. You are putting yourself and others at risk if you accept money or gifts from residents for any purpose without proper authorisation. You should make sure that you are aware of the home's policy on gifts.

Age Concern publishes a book called *Residents' Money: A guide to good practice in care homes* – see page 146. A free factsheet called *A Brief Guide to Money Benefits* is also available.

Access to files

As we have said in Chapter 4, residents should know what records are kept about them and why. You can help this to happen through involving them at the stage when records are being written. If you discuss what you are writing and can agree the accuracy at that point then there should be no mysteries about the file. It shows that you and the resident are working in partnership to make sure that the care provided is right. If you are open at that early stage then you need have no anxieties about residents exercising their legal right to see their file. You will know that everything is in order and written in a way which respects that person's rights.

The home where you work should have a system for making sure that the files are stored safely and appropriate confidentiality is maintained.

KEY POINTS

- A resident in a care home has the same rights and similar responsibilities as every other member of society.
- You need to know what the home's contract says about the residents' rights and responsibilities.
- Every home should have a formal complaints procedure but it may be very difficult for residents to make complaints. It is part of your job to help residents express their views on the way the home is run.
- For residents, keeping control of their money is an important aspect of being in control of their lives.
- You are putting yourself and others at risk if you accept money or gifts without proper authorisation.
- Residents have a right to know what information is kept about them and why.
- The care home should have a system for making sure that files are stored safely and that confidentiality is maintained.

---

9 Maintaining a Balance Between Safety and Risk

Residential care is often used as a way of managing risk. People may be assessed as requiring residential care because the risks of them staying at home are thought to be too great. On the other hand care can sometimes be overprotective. It is difficult to get the balance right between protecting residents' rights to take risks and providing a safe environment for people who need care. We will look particularly at:

- *Freedom to come and go*
- *Hazard and risk*
- *Freedom and restraint*
- *Wandering*
- *Violence and aggression*

Freedom to come and go

If we live in our own homes and are fit and healthy, we can usually come and go as we please. It would be easy to assume that a resident in a care home has less freedom than someone living in their own home. However, someone who lives at home but has become frail and vulnerable may become housebound.

What are the things which you think might create a situation where someone living in their own home becomes housebound?

You may have thought of some or all of the following. This can happen through fear:

- of being attacked in the street
- of being taken ill while out of the house

- of not being able to find a toilet when needed
- of forgetting where to go or how to get home

It can also happen for other reasons:

- shortage of money
- disability
- poor transport provision
- lack of someone to accompany and support

Loss of freedom for someone who lives in a care home can happen through overprotectiveness. Relatives and friends may be concerned about the safety of the person receiving care and put pressure on a care home to prevent a resident going out by themselves. A care home may feel that it is part of their duty to prevent a resident from taking any kind of risk. We need to look at what this means and how you as care assistant can contribute to managing freedom and risk.

Hazard and risk

Risk assessment is an important part of managing a safe care environment.

A **hazard** is something which has the potential to cause harm, such as going out unaccompanied.

When you assess the **risk** associated with that hazard you examine the likelihood that someone will be harmed by that hazard and how severe the outcome is likely to be.

For a particular resident you would discuss with them the kind of harmful things which might happen if they go out alone and how likely it is that they will come to any harm. In this instance you might well exclude the kind of risks which any person would face in those circumstances. For example if you or I went for a walk we might get run over by a bus, but that wouldn't stop us from going. It is a potential risk which is unlikely to happen. If the resident's eyesight is not good enough to judge the speed of oncoming traffic and there is a road which has no safe crossing point, then the risk of coming to any harm might be great. On the other hand you might be able to arrange for the resident to have company as far as the road crossing if that is the only problem area.

There is more about risk assessment in Chapter 12 and also in Age Concern's book *Health and Safety in Care Homes* (see p 144).

Freedom and restraint

Restraint means restricting someone's freedom without their permission. It can happen in a number of ways, including:

physical – locked doors, cot sides on beds, chairs which tip backwards or have table tops fastened to them
chemical – using sedatives
psychological – threats and intimidation, listening devices and cameras, misuse of power
financial – lack of control over pension books, no spending money

The use of restraint is very bad practice unless:

- the particular form of restraint for an individual in specific circumstances has been agreed as part of that individual's care plan; *or*
- the restraint is needed in an emergency to prevent serious physical harm to the resident or to other people.

In every case the need for restraint and the form of restraint used must be recorded and discussed with your supervisor, who will want to talk to the resident, their care manager and/or relatives as soon as possible.

Every care home should have a policy and procedure on restraint and each resident's care plan should record risk assessments for that person, drawn up with the resident's involvement.

Life is full of risks and it is difficult to achieve a balance between a resident's right to freedom and your caring responsibility for their safety. Under the law, people living in a care home have the same right to freedom as any other member of the population. Sometimes a resident who is aware of the risks they are taking, may decide to accept some restrictions on their movement.

Kim describes how the home where she works made a risk assessment for one of its residents:

Kim, team leader, residential home

When I first started working in care homes we used to strap people in their chairs but now we know its wrong. We have a man here now who falls out of his chair sometimes and hurts himself. We've talked with his wife and the care manager and his GP about what to do and they all agree that he should have his freedom. We shouldn't strap him in, which is the only thing which would stop him falling out really. It's all written down in his care plan so everyone knows what to do. As long as we've talked it over with everyone and come to a decision so that they don't blame us if he hurts himself, then we're satisfied that we've made a decision together and discharged our responsibilities.

The main points Kim makes are:

- include all relevant people in the risk assessment;
- reach agreement on the best course of action; *and*
- record the decision in the resident's care plan.

It is important to remember that it is unlawful to restrict someone's freedom without their consent and can constitute assault. If a case came to court, verbal threats could be considered just as serious as physical methods such as locking doors.

If you want to read more about freedom and restraint, the charity Counsel and Care publishes a book called *The Right to Take Risks* (the address is on page 139).

Wandering

Exercise is just as important in maintaining good health in older people as it is in younger people. Walking is a good form of exercise and many people get into the habit of taking the dog out at certain times of day. Sometimes this memory lasts long after the dog has died so that an older person may in any case feel the urge to go for a walk at certain times of the day. Mentally frail older people may become forgetful, particularly of recent events. Someone who wanders away from the home, and can't find their own way back, may cause anxiety for staff and relatives. However, the chances of that person coming to any real harm may be quite low. Often members of the public, particularly if they live near the home, will help out if they find someone who is lost. We should not take this for granted of course.

Frances, care assistant, residential home

Bob used to go out for a walk on his own regularly. He's been living here for about six years now and enjoys the fresh air and the countryside. We're about half a mile from the village and he likes to go down in the morning and pick up his pension or post a letter to his daughter and stop off at the pub for a quick half before he comes back for lunch. I'm his keyworker and I noticed that he was starting to have difficulties remembering where he was and one day inevitably he went out and couldn't remember his way home. It seemed like he had just turned the wrong way at the junction. One of the neighbours brought him back in his car so he was fine. But he was upset of course because he could understand very well what was happening to him – his mind going and everything.

If you were Frances what would you do?

Perhaps you thought of some or all of the following:

- Talk to Bob about the incident and find out what he wants to do.
- Talk to his daughter to find out what she thinks should happen.
- Arrange for someone to go with him.
- Make sure that other people, who know him in the village, look out for him.
- Suggest he wears an identity bracelet with his name and telephone number.

This is what Frances did:

Well, we had a long chat, Bob and me, about the possible risks and how he felt. It was really difficult for him because he likes to be independent and he decided he would carry on as he was for the time being unless it happened again. It probably will happen again sooner or later so we make sure we know when he's gone out. If he's late getting back we would go and look for him now and not assume he's okay. But when the time comes I'm sure he would prefer to have company on his walks rather than not be able to go. The other idea I had was that we could get the publican to point him in the right direction but Bob didn't want that. He didn't want everyone to know he was 'going doo-lally' as he called it. He agreed to involve his daughter in making the decision to make sure she knew what was happening and I wrote the decision up in his care plan so that all the staff would know. We did what we could to make him feel better about himself but it was hard. It knocks your self-confidence when something like that happens.

Violence and aggression

Someone who has dementia may become less able to control their feelings and start to behave in ways which other people find unacceptable. A resident who feels frustrated or angry, perhaps because of their inability to do the things they want to do, may become aggressive. Aggression may be directed towards other residents or towards you as the person who has most contact with them.

As a care assistant, part of your role is to protect other residents if they are in danger of being attacked, by moving them away from the area if necessary. Keeping calm and avoiding confrontation will help. Sometimes you will notice warning signs of approaching violence, such as restlessness. If you work regularly with someone who you know becomes violent from time to time then you should always be aware of where you place yourself in the room so that you can escape if you need to. Someone who develops aggressive behaviour should be seen by a doctor and may need a psychiatric assessment.

Kevin, team leader, residential home

We do a risk assessment for each person. We've got one person who if he wants to sit in a chair and someone else is sitting in it he'll tip them out. But that's on his risk assessment and if I see him trying to do that, I explain to him that he will have to sit somewhere else.

In Chapter 4 Kevin explained how he protects himself by keeping a respectful distance from residents who might 'lash out'. He was also aware that residents might feel threatened by him if he invaded their space.

The care home should have policies and procedures on keeping you and the residents safe in these circumstances. There are lots of good training courses around too on personal safety.

KEY POINTS

- Life is full of risks and it is difficult to get the balance right between protecting residents' right to take risks and providing a safe environment for people who need care.
- A hazard is something which has the potential to cause harm.
- When you assess the risk associated with that hazard you examine the likelihood that someone will be harmed by that hazard and how severe the outcome is likely to be.
- Risk assessments for each person should be recorded in their care plan.
- Restraint means restricting someone's freedom without their permission.
- Under the law, people living in a care home have the same right to freedom as any other member of the population.
- Exercise is just as important in maintaining good health in older people as it is in younger people and walking is a very good form of exercise.
- Someone who wanders away from a care home may cause anxiety but the chances of that person coming to any real harm may be quite low.
- Knowing how to protect yourself and other residents when you are working with a resident who may show aggression is important – training may be required.

10 Health and Ageing

As our bodies age, it becomes more difficult to maintain good health. In this chapter we will look at some of the physical and mental health aspects of ageing and the care assistant's role:

- *Identifying and meeting individual health care needs*
- *Mental health*
- *Help with eating and drinking*
- *Managing continence*
- *Getting specialist help from outside the home*
- *Admission to hospital*

Further information is available in the Age Concern publication Health Care in Residential Homes *(see p 145).*

Identifying and meeting individual health care needs

Some deterioration in our bodies as we get older is inevitable and one health problem can sometimes lead to others. For example, an older person having to spend time in bed because of minor surgery or a bout of 'flu, can develop pressure sores if they spend too long lying in one position. Pressure sores are ulcers which can develop on areas of skin where the blood circulation is restricted. This only happens because our skin becomes more delicate as we age and someone who is ill or under sedation is less likely to move about or naturally turn over in bed so they may need help in turning over from time to time.

Time in bed can also lead to mobility problems. Getting back on your feet again will probably take longer than for a younger person and might require physiotherapy. So without support, someone who was mobile and had intact skin can become less mobile and require extra care because of a minor problem which a younger person would recover from without complications.

The process of identifying care needs is called assessment. For health care needs an assessment would probably be carried out by a doctor or qualified nurse. For someone who comes into a home from hospital the assessment would be carried out by the hospital staff. For someone who comes in from their own home, information would come from the family doctor, district nurse and other people involved in what is called the primary care team. Sometimes there will be a case conference where all the professionals involved in someone's care meet together to discuss what is best for that person.

As a care assistant you need to know about the residents' health care, the details of which should be recorded in their care plan. The kind of information you need to know may include:

- any specific health problems, such as diabetes or high blood pressure
- whether there are any mental health problems
- how well someone can get around indoors, ie mobility and the arrangements the resident has for physiotherapy or the care of their feet
- whether they can control their bladder or bowel movements, ie continence
- what pills or tablets have been prescribed and to what extent self-medication is encouraged and supported
- the condition of the skin, ie the risk of pressure sores developing
- the arrangements the resident wants to make for care of their teeth, eyesight or hearing
- whether residents can remain registered with their own GP
- whether the home has a doctor 'on call' for emergencies or regularly calling at the home to see anyone who needs care

Mental health

About one in five of the general population is thought to be affected by mental health problems of one kind or another at some time in their lives. Older people are more likely to be affected but their condition may not be a direct result of ageing. You may be caring for people who have newly developed problems, while others may have had mental health problems for a long time. A mental health problem may show itself in changes in:

mood – over-excitement, anxiety, agitation, fear, undue sadness

understanding – loss of memory, misinterpreting actions of others, false beliefs

behaviour – reluctance to do anything, withdrawing, not eating, wandering

Mental deterioration is not an inevitable part of growing old. It is important for you as a care assistant to notice any changes of this kind and seek further help because the condition may be treatable.

The condition which we are most likely to associate with old age is dementia, which affects about one in ten of people over 75. There are four main conditions which particularly affect older people:

depression – which may affect mood, understanding and behaviour – and which is treatable

dementia – a gradual loss of brain function – which is not curable

confusional states – which often have a treatable physical cause such as infection or drug side-effect

paranoid illness – a rare condition which gives someone a feeling of persecution – but which is treatable

They may alternatively, of course, suffer from any other kind of mental health difficulty, such as schizophrenia, which is a treatable condition in older people just as it is in anyone else. We often see scare stories in the newspapers which give the impression that people with mental health problems are dangerous, but this is not usually the case. Occasionally a person's mental health problem may cause their behaviour to be a potential risk to themselves or others. This risk should be identified in the care plan so that you know what to do to keep yourself safe should this behaviour arise.

Help with eating and drinking

Everybody needs to eat well to remain healthy. Think for a moment about the factors which affect your eating habits.

You may have thought of:

- occasions when you were given something new to eat and were a bit suspicious in case you didn't like it
- being given a collection of food on your plate including something that you didn't like the taste or smell of
- spending a day outdoors and coming in feeling starving hungry and ready to eat a lot
- feeling hungry when you pass a shop or restaurant where there is a good smell
- having toothache or a mouth ulcer and finding it difficult to chew

Sometimes an older person may lose their sense of smell and this affects the way food tastes and can make it less appetising. They may also be moving about very little and feel less hungry as a consequence. Just like you, a resident may have a sore mouth – perhaps they have dentures which don't fit properly. Someone who has had a stroke may find it very difficult to chew and swallow because of reduced muscle control around the tongue and mouth. It is important for you to notice how well a resident is eating because any problems should be recorded and followed up.

Eating and mealtimes can be one of life's pleasures. As a care assistant you may be involved in helping people to eat at mealtimes if they have a particular problem. If so there are particular ways you can help:

- Make mealtimes relaxed and unhurried.
- Lay tables attractively and present food well on the plates.
- Someone who has poor sight may appreciate being told what is on their plate and where each item is. The colour of the food and contrast with the colour of the plate is important.
- Offer special cutlery, plates or cups for those with stiff joints or shaky arms. They may appreciate being able to feed themselves but be embarrassed to be treated differently.
- Judge carefully whether to offer advice or encouragement.

- Where extra help seems necessary, cutting up food may be all that is required. Guiding someone's own hand may be more acceptable than feeding them completely.
- If you have to feed someone completely do not do it too rapidly and make sure you know what they like or don't like and how much they want.
- If someone has to eat lying in bed, choking is a particular hazard to watch out for.

Physical disability or mental impairment can sometimes produce eating habits which are messy for the person concerned and difficult for others to watch. It is possible that the person themselves is embarrassed to eat in public and would prefer to eat alone. Getting the balance right is not easy. Isolating someone with difficult eating habits is not acceptable without their permission. At the same time other residents may find it difficult to eat their own food under such circumstances. Mealtimes can be social events as well as a time for eating.

Further information about food and nutrition is available in the Age Concern book *Nutritional Care for Older People: A guide to good practice* (see pp 145–146).

Managing continence

Incontinence – loss of control of the bladder or bowels – is often too quickly accepted as a normal part of ageing but in many cases it is treatable. It is important for you to be aware of the embarrassment that the resident may be feeling about their condition. Loss of dignity can happen too easily.

When someone shows signs of incontinence there is usually a reason which may be physical or psychological. Possible physical causes include:

- infection;
- failure of the body's control mechanisms (eg muscles);
- side effect of drugs (eg diuretics, which are prescribed to increase the flow of urine); *or*
- untreated diabetes.

Stress incontinence affects many women as a result of damage to the pelvic floor during childbirth. It shows as a leaking of urine, for example when laughing, sneezing or coughing. Another example of a physical cause is the mechanical obstruction of urine caused in men by enlargement of the prostate gland. Physical causes such as these may be treatable and the resident should be encouraged to seek medical advice.

Psychological causes are also common amongst older people and may remain unrecognised, including:

- loss of self-confidence and change in lifestyle;
- anxiety or bereavement; *or*
- depression.

People who feel they have lost control of their lives may fall into a depressed cycle of which incontinence forms a part. The way you can help as a care assistant is by promoting the resident's self-confidence and providing support and encouragement rather than taking over.

Josie, head of care, residential home

When they have a bit of an accident which they do sometimes, then they might have a little bit of a cry, with the embarrassment and shame of it. Perhaps they say things like: "I never thought I would come to this." But I say: "Nobody knows except you and me and I'm not going to tell anyone. And where would I be without all of you to look after? I'd be doing some boring job in a factory or a shop. So you're doing me a favour." By the time they're cleaned up they're usually smiling again.

Josie's aim is to restore the resident's confidence. She doesn't describe any of the people in her care as incontinent. She sees that as an unnecessary label which attacks the resident's dignity.

Josie's example reinforces that you should:

- never criticise or scold a resident for incontinence
- never laugh or tease

- acknowledge sensitively but don't ignore it
- be reassuring, promote self-esteem and protect dignity and privacy

Some homes respond to continence problems by toileting everyone at regular intervals and restricting fluid intake in the evenings. Others assess each person separately and make sure that their care plan records the reason for the problem and a plan to cope with it. Time spent in promoting continence is time well-spent and rigid toileting regimes rarely produce the desired result, which is confident residents who are able to manage this aspect of their lives for themselves.

Most homes will be able to call on the services of a continence adviser or the district nurse may be able to help. Continence problems should never be ignored or accepted as inevitable.

Getting specialist help from outside the home

If you work with someone over a period of time you will become familiar with their normal habits. It is important to notice any variation. Talk to the resident about your observations and find out if they have noticed any difference themselves or know what the problem is. Report the changes to a senior member of staff so that they are recorded and acted on. The kind of things to look for might include:

- changes in posture or mobility
- loss of manual control, shakiness
- loss of appetite
- deterioration of hearing or sight
- change of mood

When you talk to a resident you may find out that there is a cause connected with that person's personal life, for example a major event such as a bereavement. Alternatively it may be that a hearing aid needs checking or spectacles need attention to make sure that they are still serving their intended purpose.

A senior member of staff may decide it is necessary to call a doctor or ask for other assistance from outside. The services available include:

- the community nursing service
- physiotherapist

- occupational therapist
- continence specialist
- geriatrician

Older people living in care homes should have access to all the same health care services as someone living at home, including:

- optician
- dentist
- chiropodist
- hospital treatment

Admission to hospital

When a resident is admitted to hospital they will need reassurance that their place in the care home is not at risk. If this is a planned admission there is time for you to talk things over carefully, explain what is going to happen and provide support. This is less likely to happen when the hospital admission results from an emergency. Residents will get a lot of reassurance from knowing how hospital admissions are normally dealt with by the care home and as a care assistant you can provide that information as part of normal everyday conversation.

Homes often arrange visits to residents while they are in hospital to maintain contact and find out how they are doing. When they return they may need a period of reorientation to life in the home and their care plan will certainly need updating.

Sometimes the reason for hospital admission is a change in that person's care needs so that they may not be able to return to the same home. It may be the manager or owner of the home who discusses any changes with the resident and makes any arrangements for change. Nonetheless it will help you if you are able to keep informed of what is happening, particularly if you are visiting the hospital.

KEY POINTS

- Some deterioration in our bodies as we get older is inevitable and one health problem can lead to another.
- Mental deterioration is not an inevitable part of growing old and mental health problems are often treatable.
- If someone needs help with eating and drinking, do all you can to make it a pleasurable experience.
- Loss of control of bladder or bowels is often too quickly accepted as a normal part of ageing but in many cases it is treatable.
- Promoting continence will help residents' confidence in managing this aspect of their lives for themselves.
- Older people in care homes should have access to all the same health care services as someone living in their own home.
- Residents who are admitted to hospital need continued reassurance and support.

11 Getting Support and Feedback

Most organisations have management arrangements so that each member of staff knows what they should be doing and who they are responsible to. A staff handbook can form a valuable support if it sets out all the home's policies and procedures. There will probably also be training courses, staff meetings and individual supervision to help you do your job better. This chapter examines the following:

- *Teamwork*
- *Making the most of supervision*
- *Someone to talk to about loss and bereavement*
- *Dealing with stress for yourself and others*
- *Career planning*

Teamwork

Wherever you work you will normally be part of a team of people delivering a service. In some homes, like the one where Nadia works, teamwork is particularly valued:

Nadia, care assistant, dual registered home

We work a team system here with four or five residents to each keyworker, but with two care assistants on each floor working as a team, so that if one of us needs help, like to lift someone, there's somebody to call on. We build up a relationship with the residents this way which is much better and we've noticed a difference because they get to know our names too. This way we are much more likely to talk to the residents than to each other. We used to work in pairs and you know when two people get together they just chat and I think sometimes we got so engrossed in our own conversation we used to forget about the poor residents.

From this example you can see that teamwork is a group of staff cooperating in getting work done. Eventually you might get the chance to lead a team too, like Dan in our next example:

Dan, team leader, residential home

It's quite a challenging job but I like it. I'm a teamleader now and I lead by example. So I don't do anything that I don't want other people to copy. I suppose I sometimes get called on to do the heavy work because I'm a bloke but I don't mind that. It's good exercise but I wouldn't try to lift anything too heavy because that's encouraging other people to do the same and hurt themselves.

Dan gives us a little bit of insight into how he manages his role as team leader, not by telling people what to do but through leading by example. In the next example, a nurse manager explains how she introduced teamwork when she took over the management of a nursing home. You will see that her attitude to teamwork is closely linked with her philosophy of care and the value she places on people.

Deidre, manager, nursing home

When I took over here I looked round and saw that the care staff, as well as the residents, didn't feel valued, so I set about changing that. Many people didn't want to change but that was because they were frightened of change. I explained to them how I saw things and the benefits to them of working in new ways and they gradually came round.

What I did was generate teamwork. We have 30 residents and the home is arranged so that they are managed in three groups. Each group caters for residents with particular needs and each group has its own team of care assistants working under the support and supervision of a qualified nurse. I think it is a false economy to cut back on care assistants because nurses are trained to manage and that is what I want them to do. Of course they can do the hands-on care work but I prefer them to be free to provide support and supervision instead.

Each of the teams then gets to know their residents and feels a sense of pride in working with their team because they have been carefully selected to play to their strengths. I have some staff who bring out the best in the residents who are confused. Others work well with those who are bright and alert but need a lot of physical care. Because the residents see the same faces they get to know them and I get good feedback from the residents about that. The care assistants take a pride in how their section looks. They buy carefully selected presents for their residents at times like Christmas and have a say in the way the corridors and lounge are decorated.

Care is not a chore to them. I don't hear anyone complain about having a heavier workload than someone else. When the residents go on outings the care staff go with them and I pay them to do that. I know some homes expect care staff to do that in a voluntary capacity.

When we introduced NVQ at level II, our first group of seven got through in seven months which was a record. They have a good knowledge of what nursing is all about and go on lots of training. I make sure they get lots of praise and show that I value what they have learnt. New learning generates excitement.

Next we went on to NVQ III and at that point I approached the company to see if we could develop a career structure for the staff. As soon as we had a pool of people with NVQ III, who were ready to do the assessor training, we advertised four teamleader posts which we called Nurse Assistants. They were interviewed and selected carefully because I knew they were not all right for the job. We gave them scenarios which would show that they could take responsibility but also knew when to refer a problem on to someone else. It is important that they understand the boundaries around their role very precisely. At that point I asked them whether they wanted to stay with their current team or move on and try working with a different group of residents but they all chose to stay where they were. Their role is very important because they free up the qualified nurses to do other work: to plan and evaluate what is happening. The Nurse Assistants take a pride in their care plans and they carry out some of the routine assessments, for example nutritional scores.

We have good retention of staff. One of my team leaders might go on to nurse training and one has gone to work in the hospice which is what she wanted to do and I was pleased for her.

I invested a lot of time and effort into getting the teamwork right but they have repaid me 150 per cent. I trust their judgement and if they are asking for more help then I get more staff in. I put the labour where the care is – at the bedside. I do two shifts myself as nurse on duty each month, including night duty, so I get to know what's happening at first hand. If things are going wrong I get to hear about it. Sometimes we recruit the wrong person by mistake but the existing staff won't tolerate bad practice and they tell me.

This example gives you a clear picture of this manager's philosophy of care and her attitude towards people, both staff and residents. The main points from her example could be summarised as follows:

- Care assistants as well as residents need to feel valued.
- Matching keyworkers to residents brings out the best in both.
- Staff who take a pride in their work may reward employers by investing time and energy in creating a good environment for residents. This home created a career structure for care staff which rewards their efforts.

- It is important for staff to understand the boundaries around their role; to be able to take responsibility but know when to refer a problem on to someone else.

Deirdre is investing time and money in developing her staff and, in return, she and the residents are getting the best out of them.

Making the most of supervision

Supervision is usually a one-to-one meeting between you and your manager held at regular intervals. This might be once every two weeks or more or less often. It is one of the means by which you can get feedback on how you are doing. You can talk about any problems you need advice on and make sure that you are doing the job the way the home wants it done. It is also a chance to talk about training and career development. Some homes have good individual supervision systems but others rely on team meetings. Let's look at a well-developed system first:

> **Pam, owner, nursing home**
>
> I think training and supervision are the key to quality. Our trained nurses have clinical supervision facilitated once every six to eight weeks by a tutor from the local nurse training college, which is a big financial investment, but we want to cascade this to the care staff. All training is paid for by us of course and is protected time. It is the only way to get good quality care.

Clinical supervision is a way of helping nurses to examine their practice and continue to develop. It keeps them up to date with the latest changes in health care by focussing on the treatment of particular patients. Now let's look at a different example:

Lynn, team leader, residential home

The supervision system here doesn't work very well to be honest. There's a policy but it doesn't really happen like that. I supervise the night staff before I go to bed when I'm sleeping in because you've got the time then. But with the day staff, if you start taking them off the floor there's a safety implication. If you bring them in special, just for supervision, there's the cost to think of. We have group meetings for some of the staff, like the domestics, and I do those. We talk about problems and I sort out any disagreements between people. You always get those wherever people work together. People being people will always disagree.

Staff can always have some personal time too if they want it. Officially everyone should get supervision but really we only do it when it's needed, like if someone isn't coming up to scratch. When we had the threat of closure hanging over us we had lots of group meetings too so that people could talk about the fears.

In this example, Lynn says that care assistants can ask for supervision if they want it but if they don't ask then they would have to rely on group meetings instead.

You will find you get the best out of supervision if you prepare beforehand:

- Look at your job description and see if there are any particular areas of your work you want to talk about.
- Think back over the previous few days or weeks and pick out any situations you would like to have dealt with differently.
- Review the training you have had so far and what you have learnt from it.
- If there are particular things you want to talk about, it might be a good idea to let your manager know beforehand so that she can prepare too.

Someone to talk to about loss and bereavement

Working in a residential or nursing home necessarily means that you are dealing with death and dying. If you have been looking after someone for a long time you may feel closer to them than to some members of your own family. It is perfectly normal to feel a sense of loss when that person dies. You may want to take part in any funeral arrangements along with the family. Funerals, like marriages, are one of the ways we normally deal with life-changing events.

For most people that sense of sadness goes away after a while. But for some people a new bereavement may trigger memories of a previous loss and the feelings may last much longer. If that happens you might want to talk to someone you trust. It may be that one of your colleagues or your manager is sympathetic and is someone you can talk to but otherwise you might want to talk to a counsellor. Cruse is an organisation which provides counselling specifically on loss and bereavement (the address is on page 140).

Dealing with stress for yourself and others

Working in a care environment can be very stressful, particularly if the residents have a high level of care needs or there are not enough staff on duty. Caring relationships can be very intense because they involve emotions. You are dealing with vulnerable people who may depend on you for all their life functions. Sometimes you will be working with residents who are upset or angry and may show aggressive or violent behaviour. Relatives and friends may become upset and look for support when they visit a resident who has forgotten who they are.

A certain amount of stress in everyday life is perfectly normal, but too much stress can damage your long-term health. It is important to recognise the symptoms of stress in yourself and others and take action to deal with them. There is lots of advice around now in books, magazines and on radio and TV, on what symptoms to look for and how to tackle stress. The key thing is to understand that this is an important issue that won't just go away if you ignore it. Your employers should be aware of the levels of stress in the care home and help you take action to address any underlying causes.

Career planning

When you first start work you may not have a clear idea of how this particular job will fit into a career pattern over the following 30 or 40 years. Perhaps you took it because you like working with people or because it would provide some income to pay the rent and feed you. There may come a time when you have been doing the job for a while and you feel that you want to do something different or take on more responsibility. Let's look at a couple of examples:

Yasmina, care assistant, nursing home

I love working here. I look forward to coming to work each day. But I've always wanted to be a qualified nurse so I'm going to do my NVQ in September, then I want to go on to the nurse training course.

Dan, team leader, residential home

I've been here five and a half years after doing NVQ II in care when I was on a Youth Training Scheme. I'm working for NVQ III now and I'm paying for it myself even though I'm under 25 and in theory ought to get it free. The company is paying for some of us to do a Supervisory Skills course and we'll get appraisal training too so that will be good. But I've decided to go and do nurse training next year: that's mental health nursing, so then I'll be qualified. It's a big decision to make because we won't have any money for years. But my girlfriend thinks it's a good idea too and we haven't got a mortgage or anything yet.

Yasmina and Dan both want to become nurses but you may not want to do that at all. Perhaps you are using care work as an option now but want to do something completely different in the future. If you can, just think for a moment where you want to be in your career in a year's time or in five years or ten years if you can think that far ahead.

You may want to go and work abroad, or move to another part of the country. Perhaps you want the kind of work which will fit around bringing up children or looking after an older relative. You might have ambitions to manage your own care home one day.

You are more likely to achieve any of these ambitions if you plan your future and think about what you need to do to get there. It is good if you can talk to someone at work but not everyone feels they can do this. Perhaps you would prefer to talk to someone independent. Career advice is available through a number of different organisations, such as the local authority careers service. If your ambitions require further education or training, then local colleges will be able to help. They usually have someone who can explain the options open to you and guide you in making a choice.

KEY POINTS

- Teamwork is a group of staff cooperating in getting work done.
- Supervision is usually a one-to-one meeting between you and your manager held at regular intervals.
- You will get the most out of supervision if you prepare beforehand.
- Working in a residential or nursing home necessarily means dealing with death and dying. It is perfectly normal to feel sad when someone dies but sometimes people need help with thinking things through and making sense of their feelings.
- A certain amount of stress in everyday life is normal but too much can damage your health. So don't ignore the symptoms – do something about it.
- Care work does not have to be a 'dead end job'. Career advice is available if you go out and look for it.

12 What To Do When Things Go Wrong

Even in the best of care homes things can sometimes go wrong. In this chapter we look at:

- *Accidents and emergencies*
- *Recognising abuse*
- *Whistleblowing*
- *Harassment*
- *Handling complaints against your care practice*

Accidents and emergencies

Every home should have policies and procedures to cover all aspects of health and safety and you should receive training in what to do in an emergency. You probably know from your own experience that accidents can happen anywhere; in your own home, while you are travelling, or when you cross the street. In a work setting employers have a responsibility to make sure that the environment is as safe as possible. Managers should carry out risk assessment of all the most significant hazards in the environment and draw up plans for minimising risk. As we said in Chapter 9:

A **hazard** is something which has the potential to cause harm, such as a bottle of bleach in a cupboard.

When you assess the **risk** associated with that hazard, you examine the likelihood that someone will be harmed by that hazard and how severe the outcome is likely to be.

A bottle of bleach is a hazard because bleach can cause serious burns. It creates risk when it is taken out of the cupboard, opened and used.

What are the measures you think you might take to minimise the risk of someone being hurt by bleach?

Perhaps you thought of the following:

- keeping the cupboard locked when the bleach is not being used
- the user wearing protective clothing, such as rubber gloves

You would probably also want to make sure that everyone understands that bleach has the potential to cause harm.

During your induction you should be given information about the COSHH Regulations (Control of Substances Hazardous to Health) which set out how hazardous substances like bleach must be stored and used.

If the risk becomes a reality and someone is hurt they may need first aid. This is the kind of treatment which any ordinary person can learn to carry out with the proper training. First aid is intended to be used while expert help is on its way. You should find out what the first aid arrangements are in your particular workplace – for example you need to know which staff have been trained to provide first aid and where to find a first aid box and/or first aid room which contains the equipment they might need.

Fire is a serious hazard in all workplaces but particularly in a care home setting where residents may not be able to move out of danger. Every home should have emergency procedures and run regular training for staff so that everyone knows what to do in the event of fire. Fire drills will also be a regular activity so that you can practice what to do in an emergency before one occurs.

Accidents of every kind must be recorded in the home's accident book and some of them, such as broken bones, need to be reported to the Health and Safety Executive.

If you want to know more, your care home should have copies of the leaflets produced by the Health and Safety Executive about all aspects of health and safety in the workplace. Age Concern also produces a book called *Health and Safety in Care Homes* which gives more details (see p 144).

Recognising abuse

Abuse is any kind of neglect or exploitation of residents as well as physical violence. Sometimes it happens through ignorance and may be unintentional but at other times abuse may be deliberate. As the definition of abuse includes neglect, it can be caused through lack of appropriate action, ie not giving someone the care they need. Leaving someone in a wet bed or not answering their call for help is neglect.

Direct abuse can be:

Physical – using unnecessary force; rough handling causing bruises, burns or broken bones; restraining someone without their consent; misusing drugs such as sedatives to control someone.

Psychological – using threats and creating fear of punishment; making fun of someone; treating adults as though they were children; victimising or insulting someone because of their sexual orientation or racial or ethnic origin.

Financial – withholding personal property; misusing a resident's money; not allowing someone who could do so to control their own financial affairs.

Emotional – making a resident afraid or uncomfortable; misusing personal information.

Sexual – forcing someone to take part in any kind of sexual activity against their will or in situations where they are unable to give their consent. Under the Sexual Offences Act 1956 people who have 'an arrested or incomplete development of the mind' are considered to be unable to give consent to sexual activity. This definition may apply to some people with a learning disability.

The principles of good practice should guard against the abuse of residents but from time to time, perhaps when you least expect it, it happens. Even where there are good relationships and high levels of involvement in decision making, things can go wrong. Because residents are dependent on you as their carer, the balance of power between you is not equal. Abuse usually involves harm by someone who is in a position of power, trust or authority. Care staff in a care home are in a position of power over residents.

Let's look at this example which June tells us about:

> **June, team leader, residential home**
>
> I can remember when I first started work and someone said he could show me how to hurt people without it showing. I was shocked but I was so young I didn't know what to do about it and it seemed like it was something that everyone did. You kind of accepted it then even though you knew it was wrong.
>
> The way I look at it is, residents who live here haven't committed a crime, they've just got old. Some people, especially care assistants, get this feeling of power and use it to abuse people. If someone wants to go the toilet and you say "Wait a minute", then don't come back – that's abuse isn't it? I've had lots of arguments with one man who wanted to make people get up by a certain time in the morning. I said it's up to them when they get up and he says: "They don't know what day of the week it is. They aren't capable of making a choice." I got really angry with him. We've got one very determined lady who definitely knows her own mind and I said to him: "When you've got the courage to tell Jean Ryder what time to get up then I might listen to you about the others." But he's a coward really – he couldn't do that. He's only trying to bully the ones who can't stand up for themselves and I'm not going to let him.

June's account highlights some important things:

- Abuse is the misuse of power.
- Care staff, especially when they are inexperienced, often feel unable to change what is happening even if they know it is wrong.

Whistleblowing

When someone decides that there is something wrong with practice in their workplace then they may feel they have a moral responsibility to do something about it. 'Whistleblowing' is the word used to describe taking action to expose bad practice and it is quite a difficult thing to do. Large employers such as local authorities usually have leaflets explaining what whistleblowing is and how to take this kind of action. Smaller organisations such as care homes are unlikely to have this kind of information.

Abuse may happen just once or it may become a regular feature of relationships within a care home. You may be aware of what is going on or it may happen behind closed doors when no one else is watching. Think for a moment about a situation where you are a care assistant working in a care home and you become aware of abuse happening. What should you do about it?

Perhaps you would always talk to someone you know first, or to your manager if something like that was happening. Certainly a well-run home should be concerned to do something about the situation. If you think this is a bigger problem, however, then there are other people you can turn to:

- The inspection unit which regulates the care home will carry out investigations of abuse.
- Local authority social services departments will also investigate allegations of abuse.
- If you are seriously concerned about someone's safety you should contact the police.

If you are concerned about fraud, abuse, neglect, harassment or health and safety in the care home where you work, you should tell someone. You may be the only person who is in a position to know what is going on and 'blow the whistle' on bad practice.

Harassment

Harassment, like abuse, involves the misuse of power and can take the form of bullying or intimidation between staff.

Sexual harassment takes many forms, from sexual banter to actual physical violence. It may include for example:

- insensitive jokes and pranks
- lewd comments about appearance
- unnecessary body contact
- displays of sexually offensive material such as pin-ups

- threats for refusal of sexual favours or actual sexual violence
- speculation about a woman's private life or sexual activities

Racial harassment can similarly take different forms:

- insensitive jokes related to race
- deliberate exclusion from conversations
- verbal abuse based on race
- actual violence based on race

Harassment at work of the kinds described above is against the law and the perpetrator and the organisation could be held liable and required to pay damages.

In some workplaces sexist or racist jokes can become normal practice and it is quite difficult if you want this to change. In the first instance if you don't like the way someone is behaving or talking, you should tell them. If the behaviour persists then you should go to your manager to explain what is happening and what you want to change. If you are not sure what to do at any stage or want some external support then your trade union should be able to advise you.

Handling complaints against your care practice

As we have seen in Chapter 7, good homes encourage feedback from residents on the quality of care they are receiving. This means that:

- residents are aware and use the complaints procedure;
- complaints are recorded and investigated; *and*
- improvements in the quality of care are more likely to follow the residents' wishes.

It is very important that residents should be able to achieve change without feeling intimidated. Equally, it is important that you are able to listen to what people want without feeling threatened. It is all too easy to react in a defensive way and much more difficult to listen to what is being said and try to change.

If someone complained about your care practice, what do you think you should do? Perhaps you thought of all or some of the following:

- listen carefully to what is being said;
- find out exactly what the problem is and what the resident would like to see happen;
- discuss possible solutions with the resident; *and*
- change your practice to meet their wishes and needs.

You may need support in bringing about change to your practice because it is difficult to accept that there is anything wrong. If you really want to implement the principles of care, then change and development of your practice are important.

KEY POINTS

- Every home should have policies and procedures to cover all aspects of health and safety and you should receive training in what to do in an emergency.
- First aid is intended to be used while expert help is on its way.
- Fire drills should be a regular activity so that you can practice what to do in an emergency before one occurs.
- Accidents of every kind must be recorded in the home's accident book and some of them, such as broken bones, need to be reported to the Health and Safety Executive.
- Abuse is defined as any kind of neglect or exploitation of residents as well as physical violence.
- Harassment, like abuse, involves the misuse of power and can take the form of bullying or intimidation between staff.
- Racial and sexual harassment at work is against the law and the perpetrator and the organisation could be held liable and required to pay damages.
- If you are concerned about fraud, abuse, neglect, harassment or health and safety in the care home where you work, you should tell someone. You may be the only person who is in a position to know what is going on and 'blow the whistle' on bad practice.
- Complaints about your practice may be hard to deal with but if you really want to implement the principles of care then change and development of your practice are important.

13 Your Rights and Responsibilities

Employees have rights and responsibilities. They are protected by the law and in return are expected to fulfil the terms and conditions of their employment. In this chapter we look at:

- *Job descriptions*
- *Providing references*
- *Contracts of employment*
- *The minimum wage*
- *Conditions of service*
- *Maternity leave and sickness absence*
- *Protecting your health and safety*
- *Smoking policies*
- *Getting a qualification*
- *Assessment of GNVQ*
- *Assessment for NVQ in Health and Social Care*
- *NVQs in Management*

Job descriptions

Before you apply for a job you should be provided with a job description. The job description:

- describes the roles and tasks which you will be expected to undertake;
- shows who you will be responsible to; *and*
- sets out the overall purpose of the job, linking your role with the aims of the home as a whole.

The example overleaf illustrates the types of duties that a care assistant may be asked to undertake.

Example of a job description

Post title: Care Assistant

Grade:

Responsible to: Care Manager

The care provided by a care assistant is what would normally be given by members of the family and does not include tasks that would normally be undertaken by a trained nurse. At all times, a care assistant must comply with the organisation's guidelines and policies.

MAIN DUTIES AND RESPONSIBILITIES

- To help people with getting up in the morning, washing/bathing and dressing; helping with undressing and getting to bed in the evening.
- To make meals, drinks and supper-time snacks when necessary.
- To provide assistance with toileting and with changing clothes and/or bedding where necessary; to empty and cleanse commodes, and wash and iron clothes and bed linen (which may include laundry soiled by incontinence) when necessary.
- To provide assistance with other tasks of daily living that the person cannot manage, which may include cleaning, shopping and collecting pension.
- To record information on a care sheet when necessary.
- To report to the Care Manager any significant changes in the health or social circumstances of the individual.
- To encourage people towards a degree of independence and activity appropriate to their abilities.
- Within an agreed plan and in consultation with the Care Manager, to contribute to the supervision of people who have a tendency to wander, neglect themselves or put themselves at risk.
- In consultation with the Care Manager, to remind people to take medication, if necessary.
- To be aware of the appropriate action to take in an emergency.
- After appropriate training, to comply with Manual Handling legislation when moving clients.

- To have an appropriate knowledge of the correct use of aids and equipment used by or with people in their normal daily living, and to report any obvious defects.
- To provide general support to the client as part of a caring team.
- To undergo such training as is necessary to carry out the duties of a care assistant.

(Source: *Managing Carefully: A guide for home care managers* by Lesley Bell for Age Concern Books)

You will notice that it doesn't give the detailed timetable for each day or name the residents for whom you might be keyworker, but describes the job in general terms.

Providing references

A good employer should always ask new employees to provide two references and take them up. One would normally be from your previous employer so that your prospective new employer can check how well you did in your previous job. If you have not worked before, the reference would probably be from school or college. Your second reference would be someone who is not related to you but who knows you well and can give a prospective employer a good account of you in situations other than work or study. References provide assurance that the vulnerable people you will be caring for are not put at risk from staff.

If you are not asked to provide references then you should ask yourself whether you want to work for someone who does not ensure that they employ the right people for the job.

Contracts of employment

Employment law requires you to be given certain information about your terms and conditions of employment in writing as part of a contract. The information to be included is:

- how much you will be paid
- the number of hours you will be expected to work

- the length of time (called the probationary period) during which you and the home have time to assess whether you are right for each other
- how much notice you have to give each other when you leave or if you are dismissed
- the procedures for disciplining employees and for you to raise a grievance
- whether the home has any agreement with a trade union which you might want to join
- your entitlement to sickness pay
- the number of days paid holiday you can take
- any maternity or paternity benefits available
- what would happen in the event of redundancy
- information about the home's equal opportunities policy and procedures
- training opportunities

Employers have obligations under the Race Relations Act 1976 not to treat one group of people less favourably than others because of their colour, race, nationality or ethnic origin in relation to decisions to recruit, train or promote employees.

The Commission for Racial Equality's Code of Practice in employment gives advice to employers on the promotion of equality of opportunity in employment, including the steps that can be taken to encourage members of ethnic minorities to apply for jobs or take up training opportunities.

The minimum wage

In the past, care work generally has attracted very low wages. This has been particularly true at times when unemployment was high or in areas where there was little alternative work available. However, there is now legislation designed to protect employees from very low wages by creating a minimum wage. This will not by itself ensure that you get properly paid for the work you do. When you are looking for work it is a good idea to ask around to find out how the salary on offer matches up with other care homes in the area and other kinds of work too.

An employer can ask you to sign a declaration that you are prepared to work for less than the minimum wage but you should take advice from your union or a local Citizen's Advice Bureau or other advice agency before doing so.

Conditions of service

Working very long hours without taking proper breaks can affect your health. There is legislation now, called the Working Time Regulations, which is designed to protect employees' health. It covers:

- ensuring adequate rest breaks
- a maximum working week
- entitlement to paid annual leave
- health and safety checks
- the records which employers have to keep to show they comply with the Regulations

The exact details will vary depending on the circumstances so if you are in any doubt you should consult an expert, for example a trades union representative.

This law means that on average you should not have to work more than 48 hours in a 7 day week for your main employer unless you agree to work longer:

- You are entitled to 11 consecutive hours rest in each 24 hour period.
- If your shift lasts more than 6 hours you must be given at least 20 minutes uninterrupted break during the shift.
- If you work at night you should not have to work an average of more than 8 hours in each 24 hour period. You should also be offered a regular health check if you work nights.
- If you have continuous employment for 13 weeks you are entitled to at least 3 weeks paid annual leave.

If you want to know more about these Regulations, public libraries should be able to help you. It is wise to check your rights before approaching your employer with a complaint about your conditions of service.

In some care homes, care assistants help residents with eating at meal-times and eat their own meals separately. In others, care staff sit down to eat with residents as part of 'the family'. This will depend on the level of care which residents require and the philosophy of the home.

Maternity leave and sickness absence

A woman who is absent from work because of pregnancy or when her baby is born has some entitlements under the law. The length of time off, the amount payable and whether it is paid by the employer or the Department of Social Security (DSS) vary according to the length of time she has been employed. DSS offices normally have leaflets on maternity rights if you are not sure. Some employers will also have arrangements for a child's father to have some paternity leave. Both men and women are now entitled to parental leave (probably unpaid) during the first five years of a child's life.

Each care home will have its own policy and procedures on sickness absence. You would normally be expected to let the care home know as soon as you can if you are going to be absent, so that replacement staff can be brought in. If you have been in continuous employment you have some entitlements under the law to be paid, provided you follow the procedures carefully. No responsible care home manager would want an ill care assistant to come to work and risk giving an infection to the residents. On the other hand an employee who is off sick very often can cause real problems in managing rotas and providing good care.

Protecting your health and safety

Health and safety are important in every aspect of our daily lives, but the law places special responsibilities on employers. Each care home should have health and safety at work policies and procedures including the following:

- food safety
- fire safety
- accident reporting

- manual handling
- first aid

A checklist of care home policies and procedures is provided on page 132.

The care home where you work should make sure that you are trained in safe working practices. There are many different pieces of legislation concerned with health and safety and the Age Concern book called *Health and Safety in Care Homes* deals with this area in detail.

Care work is physically and emotionally demanding, so it is particularly important for you to make sure you have a healthy lifestyle including:

- relaxation;
- good food; *and*
- regular exercise.

Shift workers are dealt with as a special group under the Working Time Regulations because shift work affects your lifestyle and therefore your health. Working at night affects your sleep patterns and can increase the amount of stress your body is subjected to.

If you arrive at work or leave in the dark, you also need to think about other aspects of protecting your personal safety. The sort of things you might want to think about include:

- parking in safe places;
- carrying a personal alarm; *and*
- avoiding isolated bus stops or empty compartments on a train.

Local police forces or health promotion units may provide leaflets or training in skills and strategies for looking after yourself.

Smoking policies

Smoking is an issue for employers because they are responsible for protecting the health and safety of their employees. Most care homes will have a policy which sets out which areas are non-smoking and where smoking can take place. This will vary from one home to another; for example one home may decide that residents should be able to do whatever they like, including smoking, in their own rooms. Another home may ban smoking in bedrooms because of a fear of fire.

Whatever the policy, most people would agree that if someone has been smoking most of their adult life it would be unreasonable to expect them to stop just because they are living in a communal environment. On the other hand the law gives employers responsibilities to protect the health of their staff which may be damaged by passive smoking. So a suitable balance has to be found between these two pressures.

Getting a qualification

Employers often look for qualifications when they recruit new staff. The kind of qualifications which you might want to have includes National Vocational Qualifications (NVQs) – or SVQs in Scotland – or General National Vocational Qualifications (GNVQs) in Health and Social Care.

The difference is that GNVQs are usually college or school based whereas NVQs are usually work based. This means that you can study for GNVQs full-time before you have a job, or part-time afterwards. However, the college or school will usually find you a work experience placement of some kind where you can try out some of the things you are learning. GNVQs are general in the sense that they cover a wide range of different kinds of care work and provide a broader base for future study. NVQs assess your competence only in the kind of care work which happens in the place where you work.

Both of these qualifications show that you have reached a defined standard of work and achievement which is recognised by employers all over the country. Appendix 3 on page 135 sets out how the contents of this book relate to the elements of NVQs.

If you are under 25 or have been unemployed for a long time, it is worth finding out whether the course you want to study is eligible for special funding or government sponsorship. The college or training organisation should be able to advise you of any help available.

Assessment of GNVQ

To be assessed for either of these awards you have to complete a 'portfolio', which is a file or folder of information in which you keep a record of the evidence you collect to show what you know and what you can do. A portfolio presented for assessment for GNVQ might contain:

- written assignments
- written reports on pieces of work you have carried out
- practical projects, demonstrations or presentations you have carried out
- your own observations of particular events
- a diary, logbook or journal recording what you have done and your reflections on how well you did
- case examples to illustrate things you have learnt

All this material would be collected and assessed while you are studying. This is called 'continuous assessment'.

There are also tests set by City and Guilds, BTEC or RSA to assess your abilities in the core skills:

- communication
- application of numbers
- information technology

You can get GNVQ qualifications at three levels:

- foundation
- intermediate
- advanced

A foundation level GNVQ prepares you for study at the next level. An intermediate level qualification can be used either to get a job or as a preparation for studying at advanced level. Advanced level GNVQ can lead into higher level employment, higher education or professional training and education, for example in social work or nursing.

Assessment for NVQ in Health and Social Care

You can also have your care practice assessed for an NVQ or SVQ award. Some employers train their senior staff as NVQ assessors who can then carry out the assessment of care assistants' practice.

One of the words you will commonly hear in this context is 'competence'. Someone who can do all or part of their job to a given standard is said to be competent. NVQ assessment rewards competence. It also involves putting together a portfolio of evidence. An NVQ portfolio may include some or all of the following:

- written work produced as a normal part of your job, for example progress reports for care plan reviews
- case histories about specific situations showing how you dealt with them
- witness statements from other people explaining their view of your skills and abilities
- case studies showing how you would deal with other situations which you may not yet have met in a real work setting
- tape recordings showing how you work, for example of a real interview with a new resident

Your assessor would normally advise you about collecting evidence over a period of time. They would then discuss it with you and assess your competence directly by observing your work. Again the process of assessment is continuous. There are no examinations to pass or fail.

You can get NVQ qualifications in Health and Social Care at a number of levels:

- Level I is basic foundation level.
- Level II is the level usually achieved by care assistants working in a general care setting with older people.
- Level III may be achieved if you work in a care home which provides more specialist care, for example for older people with mental health problems.

NVQs in management

There is also an NVQ or SVQ assessment system for managers:

- Level III is for first line supervisors.
- Level IV is for team leaders or managers of a small care home.
- Level V is for senior managers.

Gaining one of these qualifications usually includes attending college courses or studying at home using open or flexible learning packs. There may be essays or assignments to complete. These courses also include putting together a portfolio of evidence of competence for assessment.

As you progress through your career you can build up qualifications to help you do your job better and to use when you apply for new jobs. Your manager may be a first source of information about what is available.

KEY POINTS

- A job description sets out the overall purpose of the job, who you are responsible to, and the roles and tasks you will undertake.
- A good employer should ask for and take up references to make sure that you are a suitable person to work with vulnerable people.
- Employment law requires you to be given information about your terms and conditions of employment in writing as part of a contract.
- The Working Time Regulations are designed to protect employees' health.
- An employer can ask you to sign a declaration that you are prepared to work for less than the minimum wage but you should take advice before doing so.
- Each home should have policies and procedures on maternity leave and sickness absence.
- The care home where you work should make sure that you are trained in all aspects of health and safety.
- A good smoking policy should protect non-smokers against passive smoking and protect the rights of smokers.
- National Vocational Qualifications (NVQs) are nationally recognised and assess your ability to do your job well. They are applicable to a wide range of careers including management.

Appendix 1 *Checklist of policies and procedures of care homes*

Employers should provide a handbook for staff including copies of the home's policies and procedures. The following list was derived from the Age Concern Books publication CareFully: A handbook for home care assistants *by Lesley Bell. It fits with the current regulatory requirements and is a guide only to the kinds of policies and procedures a care home might need.*

- Aims and objectives of the organisation
- Code of conduct for staff
- Confidentiality, case file recording, data protection and access to files
- Complaints
- Discipline and grievance
- Equal opportunities
- Employee benefits, such as holiday entitlements, and pension arrangements
- Quality assurance review
- Staff induction, training and development
- Trade union recognition
- Maternity
- Smoking
- Recruitment and selection of staff, including volunteers and temporary staff
- Retirement and redundancy
- Harassment
- Managing sickness absence
- Supervision and appraisal, including managing poor performance
- Health and safety at work, including risk assessment and lifting and handling
- Violence at work
- Handling and administering medicines
- Handling money and finances on behalf of residents, accepting gifts and legacies

Appendix 2 *Sample activities programme*

Date	Organiser	AM	PM	Volunteer
21 Mon	Joanne	9.00 **Hairdressing** (hair salon) 10.00 **Library trolley** will come round to you	**Knit and knatter** Knit squares for Romania or just join in for a natter and a cup of tea	Marion
22 Tues	Liza	10.45 **Jenny's art class** Drawing, painting and colouring in the conservatory **Aromatherapy** (by prior appointment)	12.30 **Lingfield Races** Like last year we have been given complimentary tickets. Picnic lunch (minibus)	Amy
23 Wed	Maureen	11.30 **Potato printing** with the children 12.30 **Musical recital** in St Lukes: Eagle House School choir	12.00 **Wimbledon tennis** Court no. 1. Cost £2.00. Picnic lunch (minibus)	Biddy

24 Thurs	Sandra	11.30 **Physiotherapy class** by arrangement in the conservatory	2.00 **Activity suggestion time** Your chance to put forward ideas for future activities (pink lounge)	
25 Fri	Pete	11.15 **Gentle seated exercises to music** with Audrey (conservatory)	12.30 **Boat trip on the River Medway** Space for 12. Cost £3.00. Picnic lunch and tea provided (minibus)	WRVS
26 Sat	Liza	10.30 **Biggin Hill Air Show** as guests of the Lions Club who will provide food and loos! (minibus)		
27 Sun	Maureen	**Minibus to St Lukes Church** for those who want to go		

Appendix 3 *Mapping the content against mandatory NVQ standards in Care at Level 2*

NVQs and SVQs are made up of a collection of different units covering different aspects of care. Some of these units are mandatory, which means that you have to include them in your evidence. Other units are grouped into options designed to match the type of care you are involved in. In this Appendix we have mapped the content of this book against the mandatory units so that you can see how they fit together.

	Mandatory elements of competence	Contents of this book
01.1	Foster people's rights and responsibilities	Chapters 8, 1, 3, 12 and 13
01.2	Foster equality and diversity of people	Chapter 6
01.3	Maintain confidentiality of information	Chapters 3 and 4
CL1.1 9	Develop relationships with people which value them as individuals	Chapters 2, 5, 6, 7, and 10
CL1.2	Establish and maintain effective communication with people	Chapters 3, 7 and 5
CU1.1	Monitor and maintain the safety and security of the work environment	Chapter 9 (and refer to *Health and Safety in Care Homes*)
CU1.2	Promote standards of health and safety in working practice	Chapter 9 (and refer to *Health and Safety in Care Homes*)
CU1.3	Minimise risks arising from health emergencies	Chapters 9, 10 and 12
Z1	Contribute to the protection of individuals from abuse	Chapter 12

Appendix 4 *Key legislation*

This is the legislation and guidance which is used to regulate the care we provide, so it is important to become familiar with it if you work in a care home.

The National Health Service and Community Care Act 1990 sets out the structure of health and community services in England, Wales and Scotland. However, its provisions were later modified, particularly by the White Paper *Modernising Social Services* and by the Health Act 1999.

The Health and Social Services (Northern Ireland) Order 1991 sets out similar structures for Northern Ireland.

The Registered Homes Act 1984 sets out the regulations which govern residential and nursing homes. The Care Standards Bill is expected to change the responsibilities for regulation of care settings.

The Health and Safety at Work Act 1974 (and its Regulations) is the main piece of legislation designed to protect employees.

The Food Safety Act 1990 is the basic legislation governing premises where food is prepared.

The Data Protection Act 1999 – anyone who stores personal information about others in a record-keeping system must notify the Data Protection Commissioner.

Further reading

Brearley, CP (1990). *Working in Residential Homes for Elderly People*. Tavistock/ Routledge.
(A sensible, down to earth and readable book about care)

Centre for Policy on Ageing (1996). *A Better Home Life*. CPA.
(An update of the care home 'bible' *Home Life* which sets standards for care homes to work to)

Counsel and Care. *The Fullness of Time, The Rights to Take Risks* (and many other publications).
(Counsel and Care publishes a range of useful books about the care of older people)

Department of Health (DoH) (1990). *NHS and Community Care Act*. HMSO.

DoH (1984). *Registered Homes Act* (and its amendments). HMSO.

DoH/SSI (1989). *Homes Are For Living In*. HMSO.

DoH (1992). *Citizens Charter*. HMSO.

DoH (1995). *Responding to Residents*. HMSO.

Kelly, D and Warr, B (1992). *Quality Counts*. Whiting and Birch Ltd.
(A series of chapters written by different people looking at different aspects of quality assurance in care homes)

Kent County Council (1995). *Good Care: A guide to the good care of older people in residential care homes*. KCC.
(Easy to read summary of the principles of good care for older people)

KCC (1995). *Good Care: A guide to working with older people with mental health difficulties*. KCC.
(Explains, in a straightforward way, how to care for people with mental health difficulties)

Laing and Buisson (1999). *Care of Elderly People: Market survey 1999*. Laing and Buisson.

Residential Forum (1997). *Creating a Home from Home*. Residential Forum.
(A guide to help residential homes of all kinds provide good quality care)

Turnbull, A (ed.) (1998). *Home from Home: Your guide to choosing a care home*. Kings Fund.
(A practical guide designed to help people make well-informed choices about nursing or residential home care)

United Kingdom Central Council for nursing, midwifery and health visiting (1998). *Guidelines for Mental Health and Learning Disabilities Nursing*. UKCC.
(The UKCC publishes a series of professional practice guides for nurses which all can learn from)

Wagner, G (1988). *A Positive Choice: Report of an independent review of residential care*. HMSO.
(This describes an important review which led to many changes in the way care was provided)

Your registration authority's Standards for Registration and Inspection.
(These are the standards against which the care you provide will be assessed, so it is important to become familiar with them if you work in a care home)

Sources of further information

Action on Elder Abuse
1268 London Road
London SW16 4ER
Tel: 020 8764 7648
Elder Abuse Response: 0800 731 4141
10am–4.30pm (weekdays)
Aims to prevent abuse of older people by raising awareness, education, promoting research and the collection and dissemination of information.

Alzheimer's Society
2nd Floor, Gordon House
10 Greencoat Place
London SW1P 1PH
Tel: 020 7306 0606
Information, support and advice about caring for someone with Alzheimer's disease.

Association for Continence Advice
9 Cranmer Road
London SW9 6EJ
Tel: 020 7820 8113
A professional organisation working on behalf of continence advisers.

Centre for Policy on Ageing
25–31 Ironmongers Row
London EC1V 3QP
Tel: 020 7253 1787
Publishes A Better Home Life.

Counsel and Care
Lower Ground Floor, Twyman House
16 Bonny Street
London NW1 9PG
Tel: 020 7485 1566
Publishes a range of useful books about the care of older people.

Cruse – Bereavement Care
126 Sheen Road
Richmond
Surrey TW9 1UR
Tel: 020 8940 4818
Bereavement line: 020 8332 7227
Provides counselling on loss and bereavement.

Parkinson's Disease Society
215 Vauxhall Bridge Road
London SW1V 1EJ
Tel: 020 7931 8080
Helpline: 020 7233 5373 (Mon–Fri 10am–4pm)
Information and advice for people caring for someone with Parkinson's disease; many local branches.

Registered Nursing Home Association
Calthorpe House
Hagley Road
Edgbaston
Birmingham B16 8QY
Tel: 0121 454 2511
Information about nursing homes in your area.

Relatives and Residents Association
5 Tavistock Place
London WC1H 9SS
Helpline: 020 7916 6055 (Mon–Fri 10am–4.30pm)
Advice for relatives and friends of people in care homes; works to improve the quality of care in care homes.

Royal College of Nursing
20 Cavendish Square
London W1M 0AB
Tel: 020 7409 3333

Royal National Institute for the Blind
224 Great Portland Street
London W1N 6AA
Tel: 020 7388 1266
Helpline: 0345 66 99 99

Royal National Institute for Deaf People
19–23 Featherstone Street
London EC1Y 8SL
Tel: 020 7296 8000
Helpline: Voice 0870 6050 123
Text: 0870 6033 007 (Mon–Fri 9am–5pm)

Social Care Association
Thornton House
Hook Road
Surbiton
Surrey KT6 5AN
Tel: 020 8397 1411
A membership organisation for people who work in the social care sector. It provides training and publishes books.

Standing Conference of Ethnic Minority Senior Citizens
5 Westminster Bridge Road
London SE1 7XW
Tel: 020 7928 0095
Provides support, training and development skills to community and day centres working with older people from ethnic minority groups.

Training Organisation for the Personal Social Services
26 Park Row
Leeds LS1 5QB
Tel: 0113 245 1716
Has responsibility for training and education in the social care sector in England.

Unison (trade union)
1 Mabledon Place
London WC1H 9AJ
Tel: 020 7388 2366
Fax: 020 7387 6692

The following will be listed in the telephone book:

- your **local authority inspection unit** (under the name of the council), for lists of registered homes
- your **local Health and Safety Executive (HSE) offices**, for health and safety advice
- your **local Community Health Council**, which represents users of health services
- your **local Citizens Advice Bureau.**

About Age Concern

The Care Assistant's Handbook is one of a wide range of publications produced by Age Concern England, the National Council on Ageing. Age Concern cares about all older people and believes later life should be fulfilling and enjoyable. For too many this is impossible. As the leading charitable movement in the UK concerned with ageing and older people, Age Concern finds effective ways to change that situation.

Where possible, we enable older people to solve problems themselves, providing as much or as little support as they need. Our network of 1,400 local groups and organisations, supported by 250,000 volunteers, provides community-based services such as lunch clubs, day centres and home visiting.

Nationally, we take a lead role in campaigning, parliamentary work, policy analysis, research, specialist information and advice provision, and publishing. Innovative programmes promote healthier lifestyles and provide older people with opportunities to give the experience of a lifetime back to their communities.

Age Concern is dependent on donations, covenants and legacies.

Age Concern England
1268 London Road
London SW16 4ER
Tel: 020 8765 7200
Fax: 020 8765 7211

Age Concern Scotland
113 Rose Street
Edinburgh EH2 3DT
Tel: 0131 220 3345
Fax: 0131 220 2779

Age Concern Cymru
4th Floor
1 Cathedral Road
Cardiff CF1 9SD
Tel: 029 2037 1566
Fax: 029 2039 9562

Age Concern Northern Ireland
3 Lower Crescent
Belfast BT7 1NR
Tel: 028 9024 5729
Fax: 028 9023 5497

Publications from Age Concern Books

Reminiscence and Recall: A guide to good practice
Faith Gibson
Completely revised and updated, this new edition includes guidance on working with people with dementia, international developments and creative communications. Packed with detailed advice on planning and running successful reminiscence work, other topics include:

- why reminiscence work can be valuable
- suggestions for themed topics
- using visual, audio and tactile triggers
- planning and running a reminiscence group
- inter-generational and life history work
- working with people from different cultures

This new edition provides advice and support to develop and maintain the very highest standards in reminiscence work.

£11.99   0-86242-253-1

Health and Safety in Care Homes: A practical guide
Sarah Tullett
A comprehensive source of practical advice and guidance for care home staff which encourages managers and owners to assess their own health and safety provision and adapt the information provided to their own situations. Topics covered include:

- UK and European Union legislation
- risk assessment
- manual handling
- equipment and hazardous substances
- accident prevention
- residents' health and safety
- food safety

£12.99   0-86242-186-1

Health Care in Residential Homes
Dr Anne Roberts
Written in a clear, accessible style, this book provides comprehensive information for managers and other staff on maintaining residents' well-being and dealing with their health problems. Topics covered in detail include:

- health promotion
- essential body maintenance
- common illnesses of later life
- caring for frailer residents
- what to do in an emergency
- residents and their medicines
- understanding confusion, dementia and mental frailty
- terminal illness and bereavement
- getting help from other agencies

£14.95   0-86242-156-X

Nutritional Care for Older People: A guide to good practice
June Copeman
Packed full of practical information and guidance, this book is designed to be used by all care staff concerned with food and nutrition and older people. Drawing on the latest scientific knowledge, national guidance and accepted practice, this book will help staff develop and maintain the very best standards in all aspects of food management. Topics covered include:

- food environment and presentation
- A-Z checklist of risk factors
- frequency of meals and fluid intake
- stimulating a small appetite
- food and mental health issues
- cultural and religious issues
- menu planning
- nutritional needs of people with specific illnesses

Written by an experienced nutritionist, this book stresses throughout the importance of good nutrition to health. Staff involved in food planning and management in care homes, day centres and other community settings will find this book a vital source of guidance and support.

£14.99   0-86242-284-1

Residents' Money: A guide to good practice in care homes

Residents' Money is a guide for people who work in residential and nursing homes who may be involved in handling residents' money or in helping them to manage their financial affairs. It includes detailed advice for care managers and staff on how to design and put into practice policies that reflect the very best in good practice.

£7.99   0-86242-205-1

Culture, Religion and Patient Care in a Multi-Ethnic Society: A handbook for professionals

Alix Henley and Judith Schott

Culture, Religion and Patient Care in a Multi-Ethnic Society is a multi-disciplinary handbook which aims to guide health professionals towards identifying and meeting the needs of different religious and cultural groups. It promotes the need for a framework of knowledge and ideas as well as increased self-awareness. It will enable everyone involved in patient care to:

- explore aspects of patient care that may be affected by culture and religion
- develop skills and awareness needed to communicate across cultural and language barriers
- examine their own personal attitudes, assumptions and views about different cultural and religious groups
- challenge institutional attitudes and working practices
- fully understand the concepts of culture and 'race' and inequalities in health and healthcare provision
- have a better understanding of the influence of culture and religion on everyday lives, major events, and people's needs and reactions.

Rooted in the experiences of people of minority cultural groups, this book provides professional carers with a unique blend of information, skills and awareness to enable them to understand and respond positively to the individual needs and wishes of patients.

£19.99   0-86242-231-0

The Successful Activity Co-ordinator's Training Pack
Rosemary Hurtley and Jennifer Wenborn
This pack is aimed directly at anyone with a responsibility for providing activity and leisure opportunities for older people within residential and nursing care home settings. Full of tried and tested ideas and handy tips, it examines:

- the philosophy of 'good' health in older age
- work, self-care and leisure
- the role of the activity co-ordinator
- designing innovative programmes
- groupwork skills
- effective communication
- making it happen
- using resources effectively

With sections on arts and crafts, physical activities, reminiscence work, and working with people with dementia and sensory impairment, this pack is a mine of information and ideas and a key resource for anyone working in this area.

£25   0-86242-265-5

If you would like to order any of these titles, please write to the address below, enclosing a cheque or money order for the appropriate amount (plus £1.95 p&p) made payable to Age Concern England. Credit card orders may be made on 0870 44 22 044 (individuals) or 0870 44 22 120 (Age Concern and organisations).

Age Concern Books,
PO Box 232, Newton Abbot, Devon TQ12 4XQ

Age Concern Information Line

Age Concern produces over 40 comprehensive factsheets designed to answer many of the questions older people – or those advising them – may have, on topics such as:

- finding and paying for residential and nursing home care
- money benefits
- finding help at home
- legal affairs
- making a will
- help with heating
- raising income from your home
- transfer of assets

Age Concern offers a factsheet subscription service that presents all the factsheets in a folder, together with regular updates throughout the year. The first year's subscription currently costs £70. Single copies, up to a maximum of five, are available free on receipt of an sae.

To order your FREE factsheet list, phone 0800 00 99 66 (a free call) or write to:

Age Concern
FREEPOST (SWB 30375)
Ashburton
Devon TQ13 7ZZ

Index

abuse (of residents):
  recognition of 115–116
  and whistleblowing 116–117
Access to Health Records Act 1990
  46
accidents and emergencies 113–114
activities, organising 15, 31, 33, 69
  sample programme 133–134
advocates 74
ageing, process of 2–3
ageism 2
aggressive behaviour 41, 42, 92–93
amenity funds 73, 85
appetite, loss of 101
aromatherapy 59
assertiveness 28
assessments:
  care 8, 9, 96
  financial 8

baths 12, 30, 32, 34, 42–43, 49, 66, 69
bed baths 43
bed sores *see* pressure sores
bereavement 110
  see also death and dying
bullying *see* abuse; harassment

care: value base 9–10
care homes:
  changes in care work 4–5
  choosing (by residents) 9, 19–22
  choosing (by staff) 12–13, 15–16
  contracts with 80–81
  differences 5–6
  extras 8
  fees and costs 4, 8
  inspection 7, 47, 117
  owners 6, 11–12
  personal allowances 8
  policies and procedures checklist
  132

registration 7
rights of residents 7, 81, 84
routines/patterns of working
  5–6, 12, 30–35, 75
services provided 6
settling in 22–24
telephones 58
trial periods 22
care plans 12, 38, 51–53, 96
care staff:
  appearance 72, 76
  supervision 108–109
  teamwork 104–108
  see also employment
career planning 111–112
catering staff 15
cats 77, 78
children and older people 31,
  55–57
choice, importance of 9, 45, 49, 74
Christmas 69
cleaning staff 15
clinical supervision 108
clothes 15–16, 48–49, 54, 66, 69
  shopping for 49, 59
committees 73
communication 10, 27–30
  and advocates 74
complaints procedures 81–82,
  118–119
confidentiality 10, 45, 46–47, 86
confusional states 97
continence *see* incontinence
continuing care 9
contracts, employment 122–123
contracts, residents' 80–81
COSHH Regulations 114
Cruse 110
cultural identity 65, 66

Data Protection Act 1988 46
Data Protection Act 1999 136
death and dying 44–46, 60
    cultural/religious attitudes 70
    effects on staff 45, 110
decision-making, involvement in
    72–74
dementia, people with 67, 68, 97
    abusive 41, 42, 92–3
dentures, ill-fitting 98
depression 97
    and incontinence 100
dietary needs 66, 67, 69
dignity, preservation of 9, 40–42,
    44, 49
    and use of names 46
doctors, calling 101
dogs 77
dressing and undressing 54, 69
    see also clothes
drinking, difficulties with 98–99
dual registered homes 7
    see care homes

eating difficulties 98–99
embarrassing situations 42–43
emotional abuse 115
emotional needs 27, 72
employment:
    conditions of service 124–125
    contracts 122–123
    first day and induction 16–19
    health and safety 125–126
    interviews 14–15
    job descriptions 120–122
    maternity leave and sickness
        benefit 125
    references 122
    wages 123–124
equality, promotion of 63–64, 123
ethnic origins 65
    see also racial discrimination

facial expressions 29
feeding someone 99

files *see* records
financial abuse 115
financial affairs, residents':
    managing money 85
    paying for care 8, 9
fire 73, 114
first aid 114
fish tanks 77
food 66, 67, 69, 75, 76–77
    see also meals and mealtimes
Food Safety Act 1990 136
freedom:
    loss of 87–88
    and restraint 89–92
    and risk assessment 88–89
fund-raising activities 84
funerals 45, 110

gardening 61
gifts 85
GNVQ *see* National Vocational
    Qualifications

harassment 117
    racial 118
    sexual 117–118
hazards 88, 113
health and safety (of staff) 124,
    125–126
Health and Safety at Work Act
    1974 136
Health and Safety Executive 114
health care services 101–102
hoists, use of 4, 5, 55
holidays, staff 124
hospitals:
    admission to 102
    discharge from 9
hygiene, personal 49
    see also baths

incontinence 17, 31, 41, 99–101
independence, encouraging 9,
    53–54
    and promotion of mobility 54–55

individuality, valuing 9, 10, 38
induction programmes (for staff) 17–19
inspection of care homes 7, 47, 117
intellectual needs (of residents) 27
Internet, the 59–60
interviews (at care homes) 14–15
intimate care 42–43, 70

job descriptions 13, 120–122

keyworkers 38, 45, 104, 107

language differences 28, 68
legislation, key 136
lifestyles 63, 67
lifting 4, 5, 55, 105
long-term care 9

married couples 47–48
Maslow, Abraham: hierarchy of needs 71, 72
maternity leave 125
meals and mealtimes 33, 34, 69, 73, 75–77, 98–99, 125
mental health 97
    see also dementia, people with
minimum wages 123–124
mobility:
    promoting 54–55
    regaining 95–96
money management 85
mood changes 97, 101

nakedness, dealing with 42–43
names, use of 46
National Health Service and Community Care Act 1990 136
National Vocational Qualifications 10, 127
    assessment of GNVQ 128
    assessment of NVQ and SVQ 129–130
    mapping content of book against 135

neglect, recognising 115–116
newsletters 72
night work 33–34, 35–38, 124, 126
nursing homes 6, 7
    see also care homes

outings 26–27, 31, 33, 60–62
    see also shopping
overprotectiveness 88

paranoid illness 97
paternity leave 125
patronising attitudes 46
pensions, collection of 85
personal allowances 8
'personal space' 43
pets 77–78
physical abuse 115, 116
physical needs 27, 72
politics, interest in 82–83
population statistics 1–2
presents, giving 85
pressure sores 31, 95
privacy 9, 10, 43–44, 47–48, 85
psychological abuse 115
psychological needs 27, 72

qualifications *see* National Vocational Qualifications

racial discrimination 3, 64–65, 118, 123
records, employers' 124
records, residents':
    and confidentiality 46–47
    giving residents access to 85–86
    see also care plans
references, care workers' 122
reflexology 59
Registered Homes Act 1984 136
registration of care homes 7
relationships:
    establishing 26–27, 58–59
    maintaining 57–58
    married couples 47–48
relatives 23, 58, 61

religion 65, 66
  and death 45, 46, 70
  festivals 66, 68–69
  and food 66, 67
reminiscence therapy 24–25
reports, shift 32
residential homes *see* care homes
rest breaks 124
restraint, use of 89–90
retirement 2, 3
rights, residents' 7, 81, 84
risks:
  assessment 88–90, 113
  minimising 113–114
room sharing 43–44
routines, care home 5–6, 12, 30–35, 75

safety:
  and aggressive residents 92–93
  see also health and safety; risks
schizoprenia 97
security:
  and risk assessment 87–90
  for valuables 85
self-esteem/self-respect 9, 38, 44
  and appearance 48–49
  promotion of 71–72
sexual abuse/harassment 115, 117–118
shakiness 101
sheltered accommodation 8
shift work 30–35, 126
  see also night work
shopping 49, 59
sickness absence 125
sight, deterioration in 101

sleep patterns 36–37
smoking:
  residents 73
  staff 126–127
social needs 27, 57–60, 82–84
  see also outings
specialist help 101–102
stereotyping 2, 69
stress, dealing with 110–111
stress incontinence 100
supervision of care staff 108–109
SVQ *see* National Vocational Qualifications
swallowing, difficulties with 98

teamwork 104–108
telephones 58
terminal illness 44–46
timetables 75
  see also routines
touch/touching 30, 42, 70

ulcers 95

violence 92–93
visitors 60, 61
  see also relatives
voting in elections 82–83

wage, minimum 123–124
wandering 90–92
washing:
  and religion 69
  see also baths
whistleblowing 116–117
working conditions 124–125
Working Time Regulations 124, 126